THE INFORMATION DILEMMA

New Directions in Librarianship

Series Editor: *Daniel Gore*

To Know a Library: Essays and Annual Reports, 1970-1976
Daniel Gore

Requiem for the Card Catalog: Management Issues in Automated Cataloging
Daniel Gore, Joseph Kimbrough, and Peter Spyers-Duran, editors

Academic Research and Library Resources: Changing Patterns in America
Charles B. Osburn

THE INFORMATION DILEMMA

A Critical Analysis of Information Pricing and the Fees Controversy

HARRY M. KIBIRIGE

New Directions in Librarianship, Number 4

GREENWOOD PRESS
Westport, Connecticut • London, England

Library of Congress Cataloging in Publication Data

Kibirige, Harry M.
  The information dilemma.

  (New directions in librarianship, ISSN 0147-1090 ; no. 4)
    Bibliography: p.
    Includes index.
    1. Information services—Marketing. 2. Information services—Fees. 3. Information storage and retrieval systems—Costs. 4. Information networks—Costs. 5. Freedom of information. 6. User charges. I. Title. II. Series.
  Z674.4.K57   1983   020′.68′8   83-5570
  ISBN 0-313-23381-0

Copyright © 1983 by Harry M. Kibirige

All rights reserved. No portion of this book may be reproduced, by any process or technique, without the express written consent of the publisher.

Library of Congress Catalog Card Number: 83-5570
ISBN: 0-313-23381-0
ISSN: 0147-1090

First published in 1983

Greenwood Press
A division of Congressional Information Service, Inc.
88 Post Road West
Westport, Connecticut 06881

Printed in the United States of America

10 9 8 7 6 5 4 3 2 1

To My Parents

Contents

FIGURES		ix
TABLES		xi
PREFACE		xiii
1	The Information Infrastructure in the 1980s	3
2	The Environment of Information Technology	15
3	The Imperatives of Automation	43
4	The Information Industry and Market in the United States	63
5	User Access to Information	83
6	Pricing Information Services and Products	105
7	The Management of Information Resources	119
8	Information Marketing Research	133
9	Conclusion	161
APPENDIX A:	The Information Use Questionnaire	167
APPENDIX B:	Glossary of Terms	173
SELECTED BIBLIOGRAPHY		179
INDEX		187

Figures

1	Basic Components of an Electronic Digital Computer	21
2a	CPU, Left Three Boxes, and Cache (Fast) Memory, Right Four Boxes	27
2b	Foreground, Sets of Disk Drives	28
2c	Two Sets of Tape Drives	29
2d	Microwave Data Communication Unit	30
3	Digital Equipment Minicomputer PDP VAX 11/780	31
4	Apple II Plus Microcomputer	33
5	Computer Peripheral Devices	35
6	Automated Closed-Loop Concept	44
7	Network Architecture	56
8	Information Utilization Cycle	66
9	Estimated Microcomputer Installation through 1985	71
10	Decision Model with Information Input	86
11	Maslow's Hierarchy of Human Needs	90
12	Break-Even Point at $50 Per Unit	114
13	Break-Even Points at Four Different Prices	115
14	Information Technologies Growth Progression	122
15	Institutional Information Network	123
16	Simplified Corporation Organization Chart	130
17	Information Services Division Organization Chart	131

x   Figures

18	Marketing Research Procedure	136
19	A Histogram of Sample Distribution by Area of Specialty	143
20	A Histogram of Sample Distribution by Status	144
21	A Histogram of Sample Distribution by Participation in a Funded Project	145
22	A Histogram of Sample Distribution by Previous Use of Computer Search Services	146
23	A Histogram of Sample Distribution by Fee Deterrence	147
24	A Histogram of Sample Distribution by Sex	148
25	A Histogram of Sample Distribution by Age	149
26	A Histogram of Sample Distribution by Marital Status	150
27	A Histogram of Sample Distribution by Education	151
28	A Histogram of Sample Distribution by Income	152

Tables

1	Computer Generations	20
2	Selected Storage Media	36
3	Estimated Information Industry Growth Rates through 1985	69
4	Selected Database Samples	76
5	Break-Even Point Computation	113
6	Final List of Participating Institutions	141
7	Mean Response to Section A—Deterrence	153
8	Summary Table of the Analysis of Variance for Fees as a Deterrent	153
9	Summary Table of the Analysis of Variance for Computerized Literature Search Services	154
10	Summary Table of the Analysis of Variance for Comprehensive Manual Literature Search Services	154
11	Summary Table of the Analysis of Variance for Interlibrary Loans	155

Preface

This book is a culmination of over five years of research in information science done at the University of Pittsburgh. It is a composite work reflecting the interdisciplinary nature of this relatively new field.

My interest in the area relates partly to formal study undertaken at the university. It was also aroused by the realization of the increased and increasing importance of information in national economies, ordinary people's lives, and its influence on human activity as a whole.

Ushered in by the electronic devices, especially the digital computer, the Information Age is here to stay. While we get excited about computers that can talk or think, we need to stay sane and tackle the issues they pose with an analytical approach. I do realize the magnitude of the problem. I have thus taken an issue-oriented analytical approach highlighting some of the leading issues. Emphasis is deliberately focussed on user access to information, for without ample access, information systems remain no more than esoteric abstractions with minimal societal value.

Some of the special topics covered include pricing of information services and products, management of information resources, and the controversy of fee versus free information. While all these are essentially human factors in information handling, the computer remains the central pivot. Inevitably, understanding trends in the developments of computer hardware and software gives us a clear perspective of the issues at hand.

Several people helped me in writing this book. I deeply appreciate the encouragement and inspiration given to me by Dean Allen Kent of the Interdisciplinary Department of Information Science at the University of Pittsburgh. His constant counsel in the development of the manuscript will always be remembered with profound gratitude.

My research colleagues, Jean Beas of Westinghouse Electrical Corporation and Charles Kanyarusoke at the University of Pittsburgh Department of Educational Communications, were invaluable in the preparation of the manuscript. As a research assistant, Jean collected a considerable amount of the literature needed for the work. On the other hand, as technical illustrator, Charles provided important suggestions in the improvement of the quality of illustrations.

I extend warm thanks to library personnel at the University of Pittsburgh School of Library and Information Science; the Library of Congress (Washington, D.C.), Main Reading Room; the Engineering Science and Hunt libraries at Carnegie-Mellon University; and the University of Pittsburgh School of Law library, for providing assistance and maintaining the collections relevant to my research.

To Janice Austin I owe deep thanks for careful and speedy typing of manuscript chapters as soon as they were ready. Her efficiency and high spirits made my writing enjoyable.

Finally, I wish to express my deepest gratitude to my parents. Without their initial encouragement and persistent support in my early life, this book would have been impossible.

Harry M. Kibirige
Pittsburgh, Pennsylvania
February 1983

THE INFORMATION DILEMMA

1

The Information Infrastructure in the 1980s

Welcome to the Information Age. The information infrastructure forming the analytical base for this text is in a state of flux and extremely dynamic. This chapter sets the scene by examining the foundation and highlighting the fundamental concepts to be explored in subsequent chapters.

The 1980s are characterized by a phenomenon variously described as "the information revolution,"[1] "the information explosion"[2] and "the postindustrial society."[3] This phenomenon is prevalent in the western hemisphere, particularly Western Europe and the United States. According to Daniel Bell, the hemisphere is on the threshold of the postindustrial society. Information, especially the new modes of its storage and transfer, has been a major factor in bringing about these changes. At the same time information itself has been modified by change in the environment. Although the postindustrial society is envisioned to be a major feature of the twenty-first century, there are indications that the tenets of such a society are already significant in the 1980s. This is demonstrated by the increased and increasing importance of information in society. As Bell explains,

> A post industrial society is basically an information society. Exchange of information in terms of various kinds of data processing, record keeping, market research, and so forth is the foundation of most economic changes.... Data transmission systems are the transforming resource of the society, just as in an industrial society, created energy—electricity, oil, nuclear power—is the transmuting element, and natural power—

wind, water, brute force—is the transmuting resource in the preindustrial society. The strategic resource of the postindustrial society becomes theoretical knowledge, just as the strategic resource of an industrial society is money capital, and the strategic resource of a preindustrial society is raw materials.[4]

As the foremost protagonist of the concept of a postindustrial society, Bell has made a great impression. Some scholars like Peter Stearns[5] and Raymond Appleyard[6] suggest that Bell's concept is exaggerated. However, among his supporters are Marc Porat[7] and Fritz Machlup[8] who estimate that during the 1980s, the information industry will be the largest sector of the American economy. It is a truism that these information generated changes are not a prerogative of the western world, for countries like Japan are and will continue to be in the forefront of the postindustrial society. In addition, some of the so-called developing areas like Brazil, Mexico, Hong Kong, Nigeria and the Middle East are likely to be influenced through contact with the western world. This is evidenced by the findings of a worldwide survey[9] which listed these countries among the top fifty importers of high level information technology.

It is important at the outset to be clear about what we mean by "information." While cognizant of the fact that the term may have different connotations in a variety of contexts, it is pertinent to adopt an operational definition. For the purposes of this text, the following definition from *Webster's New Collegiate Dictionary* will be preferred. Webster defines information as "knowledge obtained from investigation, study or instruction"[10] As to the relationship between knowledge and information, Fritz Machlup's interpretation will be adopted. He said that " 'information' as an act of informing is designed to produce a state of knowing in someone's mind. Information as that which is being communicated becomes identical with 'knowledge' in the sense of that which is known.... Hence, in the ordinary uses of the word, all information is knowledge."[11]

This distinction is important because critics who emphasize the cognitive aspects of information may be reluctant to see information as a commodity and thus reject the terms "information pricing" and "information industry."[12] Anthony Debons discussed the apparent dichotomy between information and knowledge and concluded that information is "a commodity which can be understood in terms of the laws which characterize economics."[13] The author takes the view that whereas information may be a cognitive process, in some instances it is undoubtedly a marketable product. "That which is known," for instance the current official exchange rates between the American dollar and the Japanese yen or the British pound and the Nigerian nira are absolute facts and figures except when the currencies are "floating." Such facts may be at a high premium for a corporation or a businessman in contract negotiations.

The information environment is currently innundated with what may be termed "live" information or artifacts of information. Live information may be modifiable as it is being transmitted, whereas artifacts are in a static state. To put it in another way, we are living in a "jungle" of information for which the cliché "information explosion" was coined. For the last two decades or so, information scientists, economists and other critics have discussed this deluge of information products. According to Andrew Garvin "the increase has been so exponential that we have been able to generate more printed information in the past ten years than in mankind's complete history!"[14]

Due to the complexity of society, government institutions, business corporations and individuals have virtually ceased to depend on personal experiences and perceptions as guides to decision making. Susan Artandi aptly intimated that we are increasingly becoming totally dependent on external sources for vital information.[15] Some scholars have referred to this situation as the "information overload" for both institutions and individuals.[16] Others with lighter humor have designated it the "ignorance explosion."[17] This pertains to the state of mind when for a given subject so much potentially relevant information is available out there that one can hardly claim to be an expert. Since we cannot effectively trace this information at an opportune time, we tend to make uninformed or underinformed decisions. This clearly illustrates the need for intermediaries to collect, sieve or otherwise process information for the ultimate user.

Hail to the computer and other electronic devices, for modern methods of processing information have been developed to harness and control the information prodigy. Such methods make information available much faster than ever before. For instance, using modern information technology, a new industrial technique discovered in Los Angeles (California) can be applied in a Seattle (Washington) factory within hours of its feasibility. Increased sophistication of users makes it imperative for information centers and libraries to use electronic tools. Information centers are, however, facing serious problems of adjustment. Admittedly electronic tools speed up the delivery of information to their users. While this may be a blessing for the information specialist, libraries, which are the conventional source of information for the general user, are operating under strict financial constraints. In many cases the rate of growth of their budgets is slow. Consequently, new services which are demanded as a result of automation are difficult to accommodate. Scanning relevant literature reveals that the following factors have been influential in creating this new situation:

1. Increasing sophistication of the information user.
2. Escalating costs due to inflation and diminishing revenues.
3. Advent of modern information technology, especially the electronic computer resulting in on-line retrieval services.
4. Increase in the amount of knowledge and the number of publications from which to select relevant materials.
5. Development of computer-based interlibrary networks.
6. Development of an aggressive information industry replete with manufacturers, wholesalers, retailers and consumers.

Given the difficult environment in which information centers and libraries are operating, it has been persuasive to consider ways of cost recovery. As to whether the end user ought to be charged and how much, several arguments for and against fees have been advanced in professional literature. Later chapters will explore the main pros and cons of the fee issue.

INTRACTABLE DILEMMAS

Today, the information user versus provider scenario is fraught with a motley of puzzles. Six dilemmas may be identified. In the first place, the user whether it is a business corporation or an individual is constantly faced with the nightmare of getting the right information from the myriads of potential sources. Inevitably information experts are used in an attempt to solve this puzzle. Ultimately the effectiveness of the user's decisions may depend on how efficient was the information source in tracking, processing and presenting to him the appropriate information.

Secondly, the publicly supported institutions are faced with the dilemma of whether to charge the public for information procured from commercial database vendors. This puzzle becomes crucial when the level of public funding is progressively shrinking. It is ironic that low level public funding for information centers may be experienced at a time when the demand for on-line services is accentuated by users' daily environmental requirements.

A third dilemma concerns commercial vendors or brokers who sell information obtained free or highly subsidized from publicly funded institutions. Several commercial vendors utilize federal agencies and other public institutions as sources of information used as input into on-line databases. After reprocessing, that information is sold on the open market at high prices. The question is whether private corporations should procure such information at a commercial rate or at the subsidized rates reserved for educational and publicly supported institutions. The 1978 Systems Development Corporation (SDC) suit against the National Library of Medicine (NLM) clearly demonstrates this dilemma.[18] The California based SDC had requested the National Library of Medicine to provide Medline magnetic tapes at a subsidized rate. When NLM rejected the request, SDC filed a suit contending that NLM had *ipso facto* violated the 1974 Freedom of Information Act, which allows public access to federal documents. SDC lost the case. However, federal government guidelines are not clear as to whether other agencies should follow NLM's practice.

Pricing information products causes the fourth dilemma. Users who have information problems requiring instant solutions sometimes approach information vendors expecting instant answers. To some clients, the on-line search appears to be the *deus ex machina* to cure all their information bugs. On the other hand, vendors may be facing a specific user question for the first time and they may have never costed or devised a pricing mechanism for it. Information services are typically intangibles and pose problems of whether a fair price has been levied. On one hand, the user is asking the question, "Have I been ripped off?" On the other hand, the vendor may be asking, "Are we bleeding this customer or are we selling at a loss?" Various pricing mechanisms will be explored later in the text.

The management of the new information technologies discussed in Chapter 7 poses another dilemma. While the data processing department has conventionally been the hub of most information processing, the development of new technologies has necessitated the re-structuring of the administrative set-up. Teleconferencing, library technology, office automation, robotics and word processing have added new dimensions to the information processing function in organizations. As discussed in Chapter 7, some analysts have suggested management of the new information technologies by committee. Others have supported a new management style under the concept of "information resource management."

Finally, there is the cross-national or international dilemma. Most industrialized countries are aware of the importance of information in the national economy. Information networks are being developed based on the triple marriage of telecommunications, satellites and computers. Countries are developing these networks independently, with a few exceptions in Europe. One of the trickiest puzzles is the shareability of such multinational networks. While some of the information in national databanks has universal applications, questions related to privacy and national sovereignty sometimes prevent a free flow of such information.

SEMINAL DIMENSIONS

A clearer perspective of the information infrastructure is enhanced by a brief examination of eight of its seminal dimensions: These are:

1. The Growth Dimension vis à vis the GNP.
2. The Intellectual Dimension.
3. The Processing Dimension.
4. The Physical Contents Dimension.
5. The Market Size Dimension.
6. The Information Actors Dimension.
7. The International Dimension.
8. The Accessibility Dimension.

A 1977 study by the U.S. Department of Commerce revealed that the production of information accounts for 46% of the U.S. GNP.[19] It also indicated that the information sector is generally growing at a faster rate than the rest of the economy.[20] What this implies to the librarian and other information specialists is that they have to work harder to be abreast of the new developments. The electronics-propelled "information economy" will certainly change the face and functions of information centers and libraries.

Secondly, the intellectual dimension is also undergoing tremendous changes. Fritz Machlup's research at Princeton University has revealed that at least twenty fields or subject areas are cognate to or complementary with information science "among which are (in alphabetical order): Artificial Intelligence; Cognitive Psychology; Cognitive Science; Computer Science; Cybernetics; Decision Sciences; General Systems Theory; Human Communication; Informatics; Information Storage and Retrieval; Library Science; Linguistics; Living Systems; Operations Research; Robotics; Semiotics; Simulation and Cognitive Processes; Systems Analysis; Systems Methodology; and Telecommunications (notably the Mathematical Theory of Communication)."[21] Two decades ago, some of the disciplines were remotely allied to information science, while others like robotics were almost unknown as disciplines in their own right. In other words, the interdisciplinary nature of information science is being fully explored and expanded as the intellectual foundation of the information infrastructure.

Thirdly, the processing dimension is getting markedly sophisticated. The general and inevitable tendency is to move from manual to automated processing. During the Information Age, the large social institutions will have to reconceptualize their paradigms for existence. One of the most pervasive paradigms will undoubtedly be "automate all your major functions using electronic devices or perish!" Does this mean the onslaught of paperless information systems? Perhaps not in absolute terms. But in relative terms, the production and transmission of redundant paper based communication will be markedly reduced. The U.S. Federal Government took a bold step towards this end by enacting the Paperwork Reduction Act of 1980.[22] The Act stipulated *inter alia* that Federal departments and agencies must reduce redundant paperwork by resorting to electronic information processing devices. This tendency has been augmented by lowering processing costs. As Korek and Olszewski indicated "annual shipments of computer products have grown from $5.5 billion to $18 billion during the past decade, and growth in sales has been accompanied by dramatic declines in prices."[23] In addition, modern hardware and software entrepreneurs are utilizing the concept of "user-friendly" in the design and marketing of information systems. Using this concept, designers develop systems which are convenient and relatively simple to operate.

Physical contents form the fourth dimension of the information infrastructure. Printed materials are gradually being superseded by electronic devices as conveyors or media for information transmission. Using the electronic mail concepts, interoffice memos can be completely eliminated if executives are provided with desktop CRT computer terminals. As regards mass storage, a large university library can have all its holdings stored on a handful of magnetic disks or magnetic tapes. Similarly, a large business corporation can have all records on its employees stored on a handful of disks. Such a variety of electronic storage media facilitates both multiuser and multiple access options to commonly used information.

Market size, forming the fifth dimension, has tended to grow as fast as the technological sophistication. It has already been indicated that in the last decade shipments of computer products had trebled. Chapter 8 will explore the information market in more detail. At this stage it suffices to show current trends with two of its fast growing segments.

The information services segment is enjoying its boom years. A survey sponsored by the Information Industry Association (IIA), *"The Business of Information Report,"* revealed that the information industry growth rate was 20 to 25% in 1981.[24] It is interesting to note that some of the categories in this segment are providing information which used to be provided by conventional sources—at a much shorter time. The seven categories are: primary information (including market research, credit, and finance); secondary information (databases, abstracts, directories); computer services (distributors of databases, etc.); information retailers (researchers, brokers, on-demand services, etc.); seminars and conferences; information support (information systems providers) and others (mailing lists, etc.). According to the report, of the 1,023 companies surveyed, 146 reported sales of over $10 million per year.

Another fast growing segment of the market is that of the personal computers. The rate of growth in this segment would astound any market analyst. It was very well crystallized by Everett Meserve thus: "By 1977 the infant industry was already worth about $65 million per year. At the end of 1978, annual shipments were approximately $170 million. Two years later, in 1980, annual shipments...had reached approximately $600 million...growth rates in the early years were spectacular—203% a year between 1977 and the end of 1980."[25] The information market in the U.S. is not only gigantic, but also very lucrative.

The information actors dimension is likewise getting diversified. Within the information infrastructure, the number of professionals who claim to be in the information business has markedly increased. Computer scientists, information scientists, library scientists, media specialists—the list goes on almost *ad infinitum*—all claim to be in the information business. When it comes to associations, each of the categories, computer science, library science and information science has several associations to cater to its subgroups. What it means in effect is that the information infrastructure has variegated sets of actors with different roles. Some of the actors, however, play very similar and sometimes even identical roles. For instance, information scientists and computer scientists are sometimes hired as systems analysts in data processing departments.

In a world where natural resources are becoming depleted, where resources in other countries are always sought to supplement or complement domestic ones, and where technology is at a high premium, information transfer becomes vital in international affairs. The significance of the international dimension in the information infrastructure has been emphasized at several professional deliberations. Delegates at the 1981 Annual National Information Conference and Exposition (NICE V) held in Chicago had a large dose of it. As Rita Lombardo reported, "speaker after speaker, addressing management problems, pointed to the fact that the world is getting smaller and smaller, more complex and interdependent. Actions in Saudi Arabia, for example, result in economic reactions in Detroit and many U.S. businesses. We are becoming a global village."[26]

Interdependence causes problems for which "international solutions" may not be found. Among the dominant ones usually quoted in literature are: violation of privacy, caused by transmission of personal data across national borders; national sovereignty, which relates to the control of data of special concern to a country's security; and artificially inflated data communication charges.[27] Another important international issue of interest to industrialized nations concerns competition among developers and vendors of computerized on-line services. With services like the Systems Development Corporation's ORBIT, Lockheed Information Systems' DIALOG and the National Library of Medicine's MEDLINE, the United States leads in possessing the most sophisticated online databanks. However, in 1979 the Commission of the European Economic Community (EEC) established a European Computer Network (EURONET)[28] to enable its members to access specialized information from a centralized European source. A few years earlier, the Canadian government developed a similar service through its National Research

12   The Information Dilemma

Council. The Canadian On-Line Enquiry (CAN-OLE) was developed as part of the Canadian Institute for Scientific and Technical Information, to provide on-line access to major scientific and technical databases. These two networks, the European and the Canadian, are providing many of the services which used to be solely provided by the U.S. Some observers have asserted that such developments presage an impending international "information war."[29]

Fears can be ameliorated by the fact that all participants are aware that an "information war" is not a zero sum game, where winners and losers are absolutes. In other words, no one can have a definite win with no painful losses! Be that as it may, the White House Conference on Library and Information Services, deliberating in Washington, D.C. in November 1979 resolved that efforts should be made by the U.S. Federal Government to:

1. Eliminate international barriers to the exchange of library materials and information to encourage international data flow under appropriate guidelines.
2. Provide support for the development and adoption of national and international standards.
3. Convene an international conference on library and information services.[30] Similar recommendations or steps should be taken by any country interested in participating in transborder data flow.

As regards the so called Third World countries, their information fate is closely intertwined with the United Nations. The UN Educational Scientific and Cultural Organization (UNESCO) has shown interest in transborder data flow issues by sponsoring intergovernmental conferences and international meetings on data processing. At one of such meetings the Director-General of UNESCO Ahmadou-Mahtar M'bow stressed the importance of international data flow when he said that, "Informatics...has suddenly broadened our horizons...people are constantly accustomed to living in permanent contact with worlds other than their own."[31] As the cost of computer hardware decreases especially with the advent of mini and microcomputers, some of the Third World countries are likely to be significant customers.

Finally, accessibility is a major dimension of the information infrastructure. Chapter 5 will treat the subject in more depth. In this introductory chapter only some of the dominant issues are mentioned. Perhaps the most significant questions for any society which purports to care for the general populace are: Given all the electronic gadgetry, high speed data communication and the most sophisticated information systems, will the ordinary citizen who is a bona fide seeker of information obtain it at minimum inconvenience? Who will bear the major burden of financing operations? How about data security—will there be guarantees that sensitive personal data are not handled by unauthorized personnel? While some of the access issues involve institutional management decisions, the bulk call for national and in some cases international action.

NOTES

1. Alfred R. Berkeley, "Millionaire Machine," *Datamation* 27 (August 1981):21-22.
2. A. P. Garvin, *How to Win With Information or Lose Without It* (Washington, D.C.: Bermont Books, 1980), pp. 59-62.
3. Daniel Bell, *The Coming of the Post-Industrial Society* (New York: Basic Books Inc., 1973), Preface.
4. Daniel Bell, "Welcome to the Post-Industrial Society," *Physics Today* (February 1974):46.
5. Peter M. Stearns, "Is There a Post-Industrial Society?" *Society* 11 (May 1974): 11-12.
6. Raymond Appleyard, "The Information Industry: What It Contributes, Where It Is Going, Its Impact on Information Provision in the Public Sector: A General and Official View from the Standpoint of the Operator and Producer," *Aslib Proceedings* 31 (1979):64-73.
7. Marc Uri Porat, *The Information Economy* (Washington, D.C.: Government Printing Office, 1977), Pt. I.
8. Fritz Machlup, *The Production and Distribution of Knowledge* (Princeton, N.J.: Princeton University Press, 1962).
9. Bohdan O. Szuprowicz, "The World's Top 50 Computer Import Markets," *Datamation* 27 (January 1981):14.
10. *Webster's Eighth New Collegiate Dictionary* (Springfield, Mass.: G. & C. Merriam Company, 1976).
11. Machlup, *The Production*, pp. 8, 15.
12. *Ibid*, p. 14.
13. *NATO Advanced Study Institute on Perspectives in Information Science* (Leyden: Noordhoff, 1975), p. 14.
14. A. P. Garvin, *How to Win With Information*, p. 60.

15. Susan Artandi, "Man, Information and Society: New Patterns of Interaction," *Journal of the American Society for Information Science* 30 (January 1979):16-17.
16. R. L. Ackoff, "Management Information Systems," *Management Science* 14 (1967):B147-B156.
17. Artandi, "Man, Information," p. 16.
18. A. E. Cawkell, "Can the Information User's Wants and Needs Be Identified and Met," in Raffin, M. (ed.), *The Marketing of Information Services* (London: ASLIB, 1978), p. 19.
19. Marc Uri Porat, *The Information Economy*, p. 1.
20. *Ibid*, p. 172. .
21. Fritz Machlup, "Sciences of Information: Looking Over the Fences," in *The Information Community: An Alliance for Progress: Proceedings of the 44th Annual Conference of the American Society for Information Science* (Washington, D.C.: ASIS, 1981), p. 6.
22. Forest Woody Horton, "The Paperwork Reduction Act of 1980—Reality at Last," *Information and Records Management* 15 (April 1981):10.
23. Michael Korek and Ray Olszewski, "Telecom: The Winds of Change," *Datamation* 27 (May 1981):160.
24. Information Industry Association. *The Business of Information Report* (Washington, D.C.: Information Industry Association, 1981), p. 29.
25. Evrett T. Meserve, "A History of Rabbits," *Datamation* 29 (September 1981):190.
26. Rita Lombardo, "AIM Looks at NICE V," *Information and Records Management* 15 (June 1981):35.
27. Victor Block, "Transborder Data Flow: Barriers to Free Flow of Information," *Infosystems* 28 (September 1981):108-110.
28. Everett H. Brenner, "Euronet and its Effects on the U.S. Information Market," *Journal of the American Society for Information Science* 30 (January 1979):5-8.
29. J. M. Eger, "The Coming Information War," *The Washington Post* (January 15, 1978).
30. *The White House Conference on Library and Information Services, Washington, D.C. 1979. Information for the 1980s* (Washington, D.C.: Government Printing Office, 1980), p. 21.
31. "Informatics and Society," *UNESCO Journal of Information Science, Librarianship and Archive Administration* 2 (January-February 1980):3.

2
The Environment of Information Technology

Information technology in the 1980s is extremely versatile in its applications and dynamic in its revelation of new inventions. The magnitude of its dynamism is such that even the holiest of computer gurus cannot safely make categorical predictions about its future without compromising his sanctity. Writing about computer memories in the early 1970s, Huskey[1] indicated how prevalent the use was of magnetic core memories. By late 1970s and early 1980s, such memories were outdated and MOS (metal oxide semiconductor) memories were in vogue.[2] Another case of dynamism was demonstrated in the late 1970s. In 1976 Long was skeptical about putting a computer system on a single chip and emphatically stated that the microprocessor as it existed then was "certainly *not* a computer."[3] INTEL Corporation cleared his doubt when it introduced its first microcomputer series on a chip—the Intel 4004 and the 8008 series—in the late 1970s[4] and later its MCS-48 microcomputer family.[5]

As for computing power, fast changes have been witnessed. In the mid and late 1970s, large computers (mainframes) like the IBM 360 and 370 series, Digital Corporation's PDP 10 and 20 series, and Control Data Corporation's 3000 series had approximately 65,000 bytes (65K) of main memory storage and could perform up to about 500,000 arithmetic operations per second. Within five years, these figures had been doubled by machines like the ILLIAC IV developed at the University of Illinois, Cray-1 developed by Cray Research Corporation, and the Control Data Corporation's Cyber 205.[6] All three machines perform in excess of 100 million arithmetic operations per second.

Change is such a dominant feature of information technology that given a technological growth function we may express it as a constant thus:

$Tg = C + m(x, y \ldots\ldots z)$ where: Tg = technological growth
C = change
m = multiplier
$x, y \ldots z$ = are variables affecting technological growth and can take any values.

While scholars in other disciplines can be sanguine and develop placid expositions about their states-of-the-art, perhaps it would be more plausible to consider the equivalent in information technology as the dynamics of the science rather than the state-of-the-art.

Motivated by new developments in computer hardware and software, computer applications are pervasive in modern information processing centers. The ubiquitous computerized checkout counters in large supermarkets or their equivalent in automated libraries, automated security systems in department stores and their counterparts in libraries beep daily when unauthorized removal of items is detected. Similarly, bibliographical data banks like LEXIS for lawyers, the New York Times Data Bank, and the National Library of Medicine's MEDLINE, constantly "cash out" legal or research information to lawyers, doctors and other researchers.

With this panoply of computerized services around us, we tend to forget the short span of human experience with the computer. The first stored program computer was operated in England in 1949 and the first commercial deliveries were made in the United States in 1953.[7] This makes three decades of effective man-computer dialogues. When we pause for a moment and reflect on Vennevar Bush's plea[8] to scientists to rededicate their postwar efforts to development, preservation, and perpetuation of research information, we find that many of his prophesies and recommendations have been met. Pointing to the "growing mountain of research," he conceptualized the prototype of a modern computer in what he called the "memex." Ultimately, the memex would harness and help to control the mountain of research. One can read into his vision, images of present day data banks like MEDLINE, LEXIS, and CHEMLINE, what he referred to as mechanized encyclopedias of knowledge. It is hard to establish whether the developments in the last three decades were perceptible and conscious responses to his clarion call. Nevertheless, it is important to note that modern information scientists are striving to obtain salient features of his blueprint.

THE CUTTING EDGE OF TECHNOLOGY

Comparable to aggregate demand or supply in macroeconomics, information technology has been the key element in the aggregate dilemma forming the theme of this text. Information technology is supposed to be a tool to aid information professionals as well as end users in information processing. Admittedly there may be other contributory factors; however, information technology per se lends itself to begetting four fundamental problems for the information professional.

In the first place, there is the problem of accelerated obsolescence. Both hardware and software are constantly superseded by presumably better or more efficient systems. In many cases institutions are saddled with obsolete computer technology because the initial capital outlay used in acquiring the old equipment was so high that it appears extravagant to dispose of it. While costs have gone down considerably in the last decade, very high powered mainframes are still million dollar machines. Thus buying new ones results in another long term debt at higher interest rates. Additionally, new machines may result in the introduction of new connection protocols and staff may have to relearn processing procedures. Consequently, "the end user stays in a constant state of anxiety and frustration over technology that can never be trusted to stay the same for him to feel comfortable with it."[9]

Secondly, mystique and subtlety surround much of information technology today. Information hardware and software have developed in a heated competitive and secret business environment. Research for commercial computers is concentrated in the "Silicon Valley" in the San Francisco Bay Area of California. Technology vendors are usually torn between giving the user enough information to use the machine or software and yet not giving him enough to be able to replicate it. The tendency for extreme caution and secrecy has been accentuated by the fact that computer corporations have in some cases had defecting employees who have started very successful competitive corporations of their own, like Amdahl from IBM. This partly explains the glossy well-manicured sugar-coated subtleties dispensed by manufacturers as documentation packages.

Thirdly, due to the nature of the technology, new technical terms have had to be coined to explain techniques which had never existed before. Some have remarkable resemblance in spelling or pronunciation to commonly used terms, but with completely different meanings. For instance bit, default, debug and thousands of others have no relationship with the similar words in the common English language. This jargon sometimes referred to as "computerese" is often used when more mundane words could do especially for end-user manuals. For information professionals who want to keep abreast of new developments, "there appears to be no comfortable, painless way to acquire the literacy required to understand the rapidly developing technology."[11] The problem is further compounded by the fact that different computer corporations use different terms to describe identical processes. For this text a glossary is appended at the end of the book for the technical terms likely to be misunderstood or misinterpreted (see Appendix B).

Finally, another technology related problem is that of overmarketing or overselling of products. Salespeople have often claimed capabilities to be built into computer systems or software, which are actually not as well developed as claimed. The professional press is fraught with lawsuits for systems which did not perform according to description. Some computer systems have had to be withdrawn from the market.

What this implies is that while technology has improved techniques of information transfer, it is not all smooth sailing. Making observations about technology in general, Martin asserted that "it is technology that has created this dilemma, and yet the only way out of the dilemma is more technology."[12] This may be partly true, but the technology that has so far been developed is primarily profit motivated. As long as the profit motive is supreme, those problems will persist indefinitely. What is needed is a combination of the profit motive with what modern business theory refers to as corporate social responsibility. Using the latter principle, business corporations inject more human factors in developing products than they used to do. Information technology has gone through at least four generations. Perhaps the fifth generation with more educated users, and tougher competition will see systems which are more user oriented.

COMPUTER GENERATIONS

Of the five computer generations that may be identified (see Table 1), the first three are distinctive and clearly demarcated. This is due to

The Environment of Information Technology   19

the considerably different technologies they used in computer components. On the other hand, the distinction between the fourth and the fifth appears to be based on degrees of development of the same technology. In fact while some scientists have claimed that we are at the threshold of the fifth generation computer, others refute the assertion and point out that fourth generation computers are still in their adolescence. Thus they argue that we cannot possibly be in the fifth generation. As will be discussed later, current research in Japan and the United States indicates that information processing is about to take a new turn. It appears that new features of data processing, which will be based on what are called very large scale integrated circuits (VLSI), will certainly catapult information professionals into the fifth generation computer age.[13]

At the analytical level, a brief review of computer generations helps our understanding of modern data processing. The perspective thus created enhances our attempt to explain several developmental issues and questions. Among such questions are: Why were earlier generations of computers not technically suitable for use in information centers and libraries? Why were they so expensive? On the other side of the coin, why are modern computers relatively cheaper and more accessible to information centers and libraries? What are the probable consequences of fifth generation computers on libraries and information centers? Using a quasi analytico-history of science method, can we extrapolate and envision the future through a crystal ball?

A computer is essentially no more than a conglomeration of a very large number of electronic circuits arranged in a logical manner to perform specific functions. Circuits are grouped by what they can do to make the functional components of the computer system. There is a clearly defined division of labor in the information processing world. While the electronics engineer takes care of the minutiae of circuit design, other professionals like computer scientists, information scientists, and librarians are more concerned with the functions of the various components of the computer. The latter groups' main interest is the contribution of the components to effective data and information processing.

Through the generations, the core of a computer system has maintained the same basic structure or "architecture" as shown in Figure 1. This is a very simplified picture of a computer system. Modern computers may differ in the sophistication of the components, size or

Generation	Period of Major Use	Major Characteristics
First	1953–1949	Vacuum tubes technology. Hollerith card reader, card punch input/output devices. No operating systems; magnetic core memories. High heat emission, bulky.
Second	1959–1964	Transistor technology. Magnetic tape, line printer, magnetic disks, input/output devices. Primitive operating systems. Low heat emission.
Third	1964–1972	Integrated circuits technology. Sophisticated operating systems. On line and time sharing systems. 　Minicomputers 　Optical character recognition 　Multiprocessing and multiprogramming 　Graphic terminals
Fourth	1972–1980	Large scale integration technology. 　Teleprocessing 　View data, videotext, animation 　Very sophisticated operating systems 　Microcomputers 　Artificial intelligence, robots 　Distributed processing
Fifth	1980 +	Very large scale integration technology. Very sophisticated operating systems. 　Voice recognition 　More sophisticated artificial intelligence applications

Table 1. Computer Generations

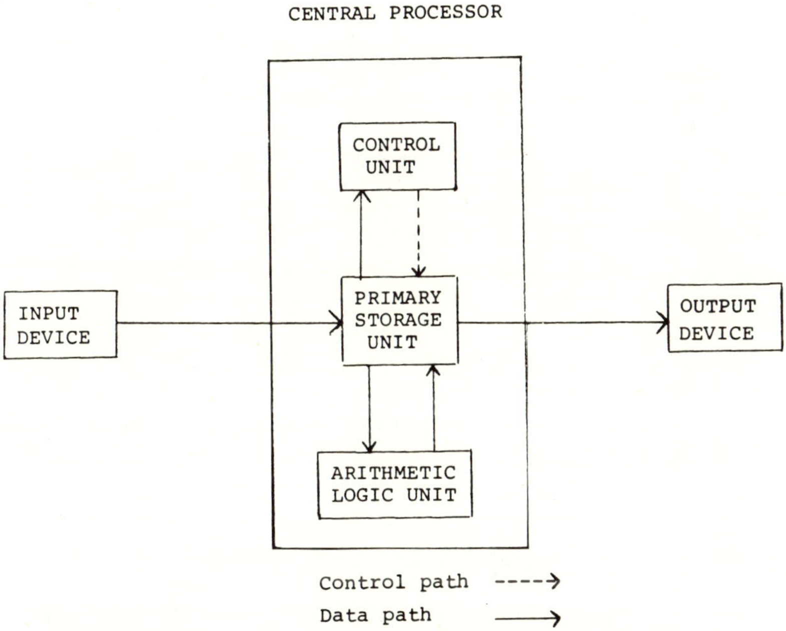

The Environment of Information Technology   21

CENTRAL PROCESSOR

```
                    ┌──────────┐
                    │ CONTROL  │
                    │   UNIT   │
                    └──────────┘
                         ↑
                         ¦
                         ↓
┌────────┐          ┌──────────┐          ┌────────┐
│ INPUT  │ ───────→ │ PRIMARY  │ ───────→ │ OUTPUT │
│ DEVICE │          │ STORAGE  │          │ DEVICE │
└────────┘          │   UNIT   │          └────────┘
                    └──────────┘
                         ↑
                         ↓
                    ┌──────────┐
                    │ ARITHMETIC│
                    │ LOGIC UNIT│
                    └──────────┘
```

Control path ---->
Data path   ———→

Figure 1. Basic Components of an Electronic Digital Computer

power. In all configurations, however, the central processor is the "computer" performing five basic functions using the following components:

1. *Control Unit* which is the main commanding force within the system and (a) instructs the input devices when and what data to enter into the primary storage unit; (b) instructs the primary storage unit how the data is going to be stored; (c) instructs the arithmetic logic unit what computations to execute and where to locate the results; (d) instructs the output devices how to receive and display the results of a processed task.
2. *Input Device* which accepts and transmits data to be processed to the central processor. A variety of such devices exists in modern computer configurations.
3. *Primary Storage Unit* which is a sort of general purpose "scratch area" of the computer where data to be processed is kept. Permanent storage is normally achieved through what are called auxilliary or secondary storage systems (magnetic disks, drums, tapes, microforms, etc.).
4. *Arithmetic Logic Unit* which allows the computer to make decisions based on mathematical instructions called algorithms. It also performs the basic

mathematical functions of addition, multiplication, division or subtraction. When data to be manipulated is completed, it is returned to the primary storage unit.
5. *Output Device* which accepts and displays processed data to the end user. Like input devices, there is currently a very large variety of output devices. Modern computer designers spend a lot of time on both output and input devices to make computers user-friendly.

While the precise dates may be blurred by overlapping inventions, professional opinion indicates that first generation computers came to the public scene in the 1950s. "Generation" implicitly refers to commercial deliveries and general public acceptance. Table 1 shows the five main generations and their characteristics. The ENIAC (Electronic Numerical Integrator and Calculator), built at the University of Pennsylvania, and the EDSAC (Electronic Delay Storage Automatic Calculator) built at Cambridge University in England, were some of the first electronic computers.[14] Among the commercial deliveries, IBM, Monroe, NCR, Burroughs, RCA, Underwood and UNIVAC were the main manufacturers. IBM was in the forefront with its 650 and 700 series.[15] The key electronic component was the electronic vacuum tube, which was used as the main counting device. A typical first generation computer executed about 1,000 instructions per second and had a storage capacity of approximately 10,000 to 20,000 (10-20K) characters of data in its primary or main memory.

Although the ENIAC was not commercially produced, it demonstrated most of the characteristics of machines of the time. Working jointly, John W. Mauchly and J. Presper Eckert invented and built this prototype. By modern standards it was a gigantic machine, which weighed about 30 tons, occupied 1500 square feet, contained about 19,000 vacuum tubes and used 130 Kilowatts of power. It used so much power that stories run that people in West Philadelphia could tell it was switched on when their lights dimmed.

Typically, first generation computers were bulky, used enormous electric power and were used for scientific and mathematical computations. Most important, they did not have an operating system which is invaluable in job scheduling in present day multi-user environments.

The second generation of computers was ushered in by the use of transistors instead of vacuum tubes. Although invented by physicists in 1947 at Bell Laboratories in New Jersey, it was not until the late 1950s and 1960s that transistors were widely used in computers. In contrast to vacuum tubes, transistors use solids as the medium in which electronic functions occur. Consequently they were the first so called solid-state electronic devices. Transistors were much faster, smaller, more reliable and required less power than the vacuum tubes. While the first generation's speeds were measured in milli-seconds (thousandths of a second) second generation machines had improved by a factor of 1,000 to 1,000,000 instructions per second, thus performing at microsecond speeds (one millionth of a second per instruction). As regards main memory capacity, they had in excess of 65,000 (65K) storage locations. Among the commercial machines on the market were Honeywell 800, Burroughs B5500, UNIVAC 1107, IBM 1400, IBM 7090 and Control Data Corporation 1604.

In addition to solid-state devices, second generation machines had other improvements. They used operating systems, time sharing and user oriented languages. They were still scientifically oriented with the processor and memory occupying 60-70% of the whole machine configuration. Thus reading cards and producing reports, which are a library's or information center's normal requirements were considered wasteful.[16]

The third generation of computers came around 1964. It was the result of the invention of the integrated circuit in 1957.[17] Typically an integrated circuit (IC) is a device that combines the capabilities of many transistors and other circuit components on one tiny silicon chip (approximately 1/16 × 1/16 of an inch). Using integrated circuits as basic building elements, computers which are much faster, with larger memories have been constructed. Third generation computers were characterized by speeds of 10 million additions per second and main memories of over 10 million storage locations. IBM's System/360 and System/370 were the dominant machines of the generation. Most of the other major manufacturers like Control Data Corporation, Burroughs, Honeywell, UNIVAC and NCR had representative products.

The use of integrated circuits during the third generation resulted in the decrease in the size of computer components. Consequently minicomputers became popular in the mid-1970s. Digital Equipment Corporation was leader in the market with its PDP 11 series computers. Other corporations included Texas Instruments, NCR, Apple Computer Inc. and Tandy Corporation (Radio Shack.)

Fourth generation computers came onto the scene in the late 1970s with increased density of integrated circuits. This led to what has been referred to as LSIs (Large Scale Integrated Circuits). The physical size of systems has been reduced remarkably while performance has increased. The 1970s computer scene became complex due to the systems that were available. Mainframes, minicomputers and later microcomputers vied for attention and market share. Multiprocessing, multiprogramming and virtual memory concepts became important in computer systems design. Multiprocessing implies using more than one central processor in the computer system configuration. Multiprogramming is using paging (partial processing) and fitting more jobs or program executions into a given time period. On the other hand, virtual memory implies manipulation of computer primary and secondary memories to make it appear as if more memory were available to the user than what is actually allocated to him. Among the typical fourth generation large computers is the Amdahl 580-5860 which uses ECL/LSI (Emitter Coupled Logic/Large Scale Integrated) chips as building blocks.[18] Many of the minicomputer manufacturers like Digital Equipment Corporation, Datapoint, and Data General have also used LSI circuits to design their computers. Typically, the largest of the fourth generation computers have a basic memory size of 16M bytes which can be increased by increments of 8M to a maximum of 32M bytes. As regards processing speeds, they range from 10 to about 16 million instructions per second (MIPS).

Finally, the fifth generation of computer systems may originate from Japan whose Ministry of International Trade & Industry (MITI) proposes to spend $44.5 million over a ten year period to plunge into computer systems leadership.[19] Three separate areas of computing are likely to be brought together within the next decade.[20] In the first place, what are called expert systems—which can mimic the human mind—are to be designed to perform several functions currently performed by humans. This concept is within the realm of artificial intelligence and advanced use of computer-operated robots. Secondly, distributed processing will combine several computer systems and subsystems. Minis, micros and mainframes will be programmed to perform coordinated tasks. Finally, the use of very large scale integration (VLSI) will result in the feasibility of the first and second concepts at reasonable costs. It is very likely that during the fifth generation of computer systems, robots may be able to operate some sections of information centers and libraries and dish out packages of information in lieu of human operators!

CURRENT TRENDS IN COMPUTER TECHNOLOGY

Early computer systems designers concentrated on developing a very powerful central processing unit (CPU) and paid less attention to peripheral devices that perform input and output functions. This early trend was due to three basic reasons. First, because electronic components were very expensive it was a virtue to minimize component count.[21] Secondly, early machines were designed to facilitate scientific mathematical computations. Consequently text searching, comprehensive report generation and multi-user interfaces, which require sophisticated peripherals were scarcely supported. Finally, the operating systems available did not have the capabilities necessary to permit the interconnection of several components.

Today, software houses and computer manufacturers have developed very sophisticated operating systems which have made it possible to "hang" several devices on a single computer system. In addition, partly due to the development of very large scale integrated circuits (VLSI), component costs have been remarkably reduced. Costs have been reduced at a magnitude of 10^{-3} per bit within the last five years.[22] This tendency has been accentuated by very high demand for computer services—generated by availability of online services.

As a result, an upward moving self perpetuating spiral effect is created whereby more demand begets better services and machines, which calls for more demand. Equipment and services become cheaper due to the economies of scale. Current designs are thus more storage-oriented and give more attention to storage devices and their interconnection.

Presently, three main types of computers may be categorized: the large scale mainframes, minicomputers and microcomputers. Some industry analysts have argued that there is another category worth noting, the midicomputers; however that category has not been as popular as the other computer classifications. Analysis of these classes has to be handled with caution. A decade or so ago it was easy to classify a given computer and put it in these almost discrete groups or slots according to, say, word size, speed, memory size, operating system, programming languages used and functional capabilities. Current developments have blurred these distinctions. Miller clearly characterized the confused situation caused by "the introduction of microcomputers, LSI versions of minicomputers and larger, more powerful minicomputers, and minicomputer-size mainframes."[23]

Until the 1960s, large-scale computer systems—the mainframes—were paramount in the data processing arena. Figures 2a-d show the PDP System 10 mainframe components at the University of Pittsburgh Central Computer Facility. They are generally characterized by large magnitudes of speed, memory capacity, cost, and number of peripherals supported. For instance, cycle times (time to perform an operation) for mainframes range from 10-100 ns (ns = nanosecond—one billionth of a second) compared to minis with 500-900 ns. Some of the latest giant mainframes—Amdahl 580-5860, IBM 3081 and National Advanced Systems's AS/9000 DPC far surpass the minis in almost all magnitudes.[24] This class of giants have expandable main memories up to 32M bytes and speeds of 11-16 MIPS (million instructions per second). Their prices range from $4.3 million to $5.5 millon. To the information scientist and librarian, the advent of such high powered machines implies that nationwide data banks and networks like Dow Jones, OCLC, MEDLINE and Electronic Fund Transfer (EFT) systems for banking institutions, become more effective.

One of the main identifying characteristics for minicomputers used to be the word length—typically 8, 12 or 16 bits. In contrast, large mainframes used to boast of 32-36 bit words—for instance, IBM 360 and 370 have 32-bit word length; Univac 1100 and Digital Equipment Corporation (DEC) PDP 10 had 36-bit words. In the late seventies, "super" minicomputers were marketed with 32-bit word length. Examples include Data General's MV/8000 and DEC 11/780 of the VAX family. Figure 3 shows the DEC PDP 11/780 VAX at IDIS information laboratory at the University of Pittsburgh.

Other new features that make minis act like large mainframes include a wider range of programming languages, powerful and sophisticated operating systems, high-level performance data base management systems (DBMS) and relatively large main memory sizes 128-512K bytes. This tendency has been dubbed by Miller as "growing up" into a mainframe.[25] It is important to note that this is happening with prices which are much lower than the larger machines. For instance it is possible to have a stand alone minicomputer system with prices ranging from $100,000-$400,000. At such a price the package would include a processor, memory, disk and tape drives, storage subsystems, a printer and several CRT (Cathode Ray Tube) terminals. This implies that some

Figure 2a. CPU, Left Three Boxes, and Cache (Fast) Memory, Right Four Boxes

Figure 2b. Foreground, Sets of Disk Drives

Figure 2c. Two Sets of Tape Drives

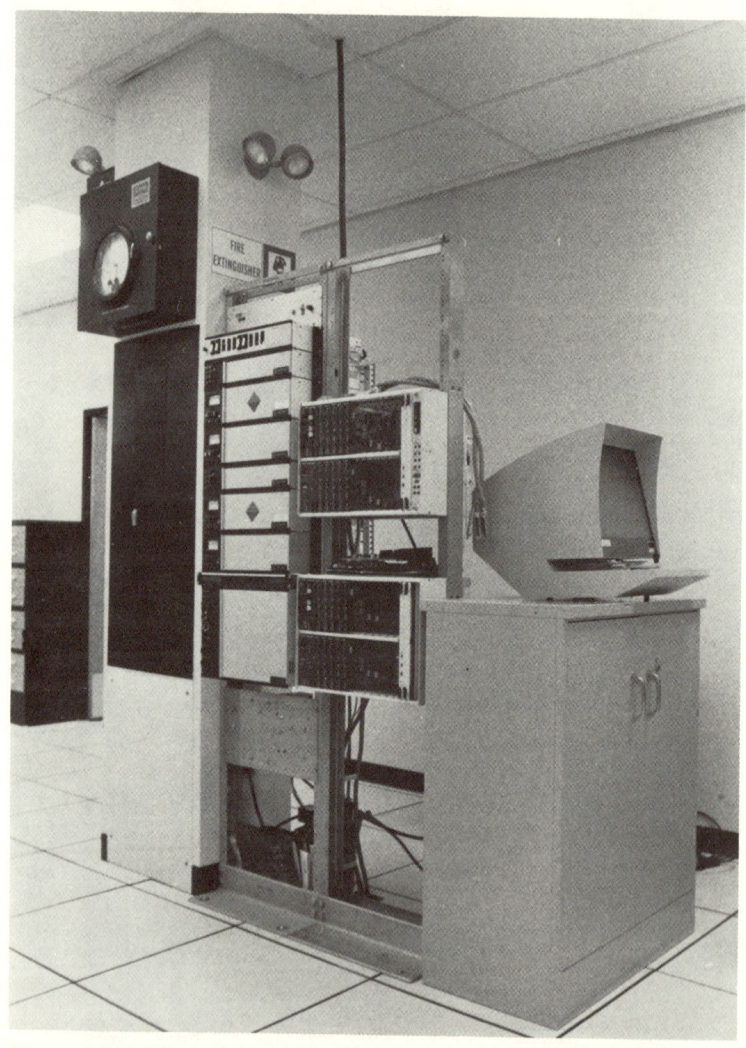

Figure 2d. Microwave Data Communication Unit

Figure 3. Digital Equipment Minicomputer PDP VAX 11/780

libraries and information centers can have their own systems, independent of the parent institutions, at reasonable prices and yet have the efficiency comparable to large computers.

The last category of the troika is the microcomputer, which so far illustrates adept miniaturization of computers using the latest LSI and VLSI technology. VLSI and the development of microcomputers appear to promise a boon for information professionals. For instance, Apple IIe computer with minimal peripheral devices costs $2,000. This implies that even some of the poorly financed information centers would in the future use micros to automate at least some of their housekeeping functions. According to Mead and Conway,

> Many LSI chips, such as microprocessors now consist of multiple computer subsystems, and thus really integrated systems microcomputers rather than integrated circuits.... Physical principles indicate that transistors can be scaled down to less than 1/100th of their present area and still function as sort of switching elements with which we can build digital systems. By the late 1980s it will be possible to fabricate chips containing millions of transistors.[26]

Microcomputers have typically been manufactured as 8-bit and 16-bit word machines. Figure 4 shows an Apple II Plus microcomputer manufactured by Apple Computer Inc.

In 1981, Hewlett-Packard and INTEL Corporation announced the development and production of 32-bit microcomputers.[27] When these machines get to the market in the 1980s, classification and categorization will indeed be confused. The HP system contains a chip with 450,000 MOS (metal oxide semiconductor) devices. The combination of large scale mainframes, minicomputers, and microcomputers has resulted in complex multiprocessing multiuser information systems. The 1980s will certainly see an improvement in their efficiency and an expansion in services provided.

THE ROLE OF MASS STORAGE TECHNOLOGY

One of the most influential aspects of information technology of special relevance to the information specialist and librarian is the development of mass storage devices for computer systems. As Figure 5 indicates, they may be used in either the input or output functions of a

Figure 4. Apple II Plus Microcomputer

computer system. These devices are sometimes referred to as input-output (I/O) devices or simply as peripherals. Their importance to information scientists is highlighted by noting that by the nature of their jobs, they need a lot of information stored and retrieved preferably on line. Whereas scientific data processing needs more central processor time, information processing for libraries and information centers requires manipulation of data on peripherals in store-retrieve mode—usually referred to as input-output (I/O) mode. The devices are divided into two basic categories, random (or direct) and sequential access. The former implies ability to access any record on the device as required and the latter implies access only sequentially from beginning to end. Among institutions which have taken advantage of large scale mass storage are OCLC, BALLOTS, and Systems Development Corporation, to mention only a few. When in 1981 the Library of Congress decided to replace its card catalog with an on-line computerized catalog, it acquired 6 billion bytes of mass storage.[28]

Magnetic tape is among the oldest media and has one of the highest storage capacities. Due to its sequential access, however, it has limited usefulness for on-line storage systems. Punched cards are another medium within the sequential access type that have been used extensively in data processing. They too have the drawback of inability to be manipulated conveniently on line. Table 2 shows comparisons of the commonly used media.

With the increased and increasing use of on-line services, random access devices are becoming more popular in information processing. Among the most common are magnetic disks, magnetic drums and floppy disks. While cognizant of the rate of obsolescence of definite statistical specifications, it may be noted that one of the latest disks by IBM has some of the highest storage capacities. The IBM 3380 has a storage capacity of 2.52 gigabytes of on-line storage per unit or 10.18 gigabytes per disk pack of four (a gigabyte is 1,000 megabytes or one billion bytes).[29]

Finally, another mass medium is the Computer Output Microfilm (COM). This is made when data from the central processor is read into a microfilm recorder connected to a film developer. The final microfilm output may be either on microfiche or on a microfilm. COM is becoming popular for storing archival material which used to be kept on magnetic tapes. Its advantage over the magnetic tape is that it does not deteriorate as fast as the tape.

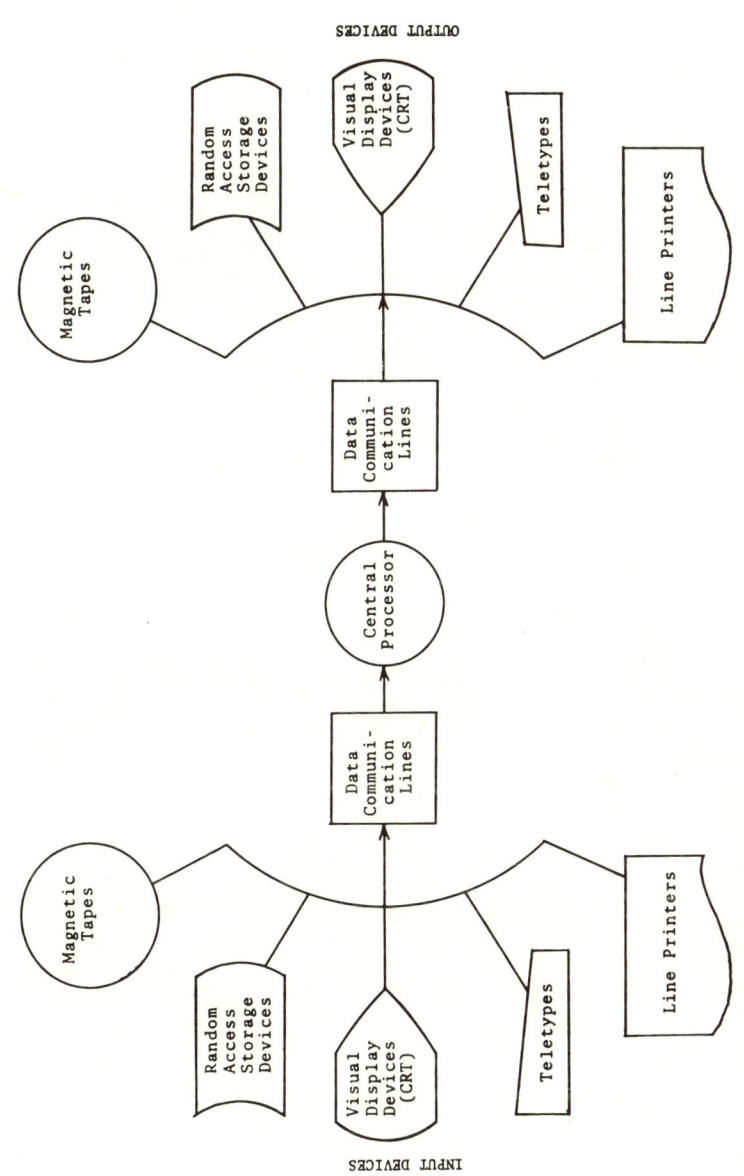

Figure 5. Computer Peripheral Devices

	MEDIUM						
	MOS MEMORY UNITS	MAGNETIC DRUM	MAGNETIC DISK	BUBBLE MEMORY	PUNCHED CARDS	MAGNETIC TAPE	FLOPPY DISK
TYPE OF STORAGE	Primary Random Access	Secondary Semi Random Access	Secondary Semi Random Access	Secondary Semi Random Access	Sequential	Sequential	Semi Random Access
CAPACITY**	2 (64,000/chip)	2	10.08	0.1 per chip	0.16 per box	46	0.25
TRANSFER RATE*	2	1	0.16	2	0.0018	0.4	0.4
ACCESS TIME/SEC	1/2000000	1/100	1/80	1/3000	12 (assuming 500 cards in hopper)	50	1/40
HARDWARE COST ***	7	800	10,000	30	100	90,000	3,000

* Million characters per second
** Million characters
*** Bits per penny

Table 2. Selected Storage Media

DATA ENTRY AND DISPLAY

Ingenuity and resourcefulness are currently being utilized in designing data entry and display devices more amenable to human comfort. In the earlier generations of computers, the computer industry paid little attention to man-computer dialogues.[30] With the use of human oriented design technique called ergonomics has come improved appearance and ease of use of computer terminals and other display devices.

Alphanumeric terminals usually known as teletypes are some of the most common terminals. Their keyboards are similar to the ordinary typewriter and have hard-copy outputs. The latter characteristic is one of their major advantages over some of the Cathode Ray Tube (CRT) terminals which do not have this facility.

CRTs are increasing in popularity partly due to their visual images and due to the fact that attachments can be bought to facilitate hard-copy productions. In addition, color graphics—whereby charts or graphs are neatly drawn on the CRT on request—make them particularly attractive. Some terminals can display eight color images.[31]

Tremendous developments have been made in optical character recognition (OCR) whereby a variety of devices are used to read in data without typing. Electronically sensitive wands or light pens are now used in libraries and information centers to record readers and books details. It is interesting to note how devices which originally started in business have successfully been adopted for library use. For instance several libraries now use the Universal Product Code (UPC) concept in recording items checked out of the library. Information is pre-recorded about the book on a UPC label pasted on the book. At the lending time reader and book details are matched using a light pen and a charge is automatically recorded in the system's mass storage.

Finally, the 1980s are witnessing rapid developments in printer technology. According to Williams there were 1,250 different printers on the market in 1981.[32] These printers were using 10-15 different technologies. Among the latest are laser printers which can print 10-215 pages per minute. Of special interest to an information specialist is the fact that the printers are improving in speed, variety of fonts (typefaces), and quality of products printed.

DATA COMMUNICATIONS AND NETWORKS

The French call it "telematique"[33] which when Americanized becomes telematic. Some American scholars have termed it

38 The Information Dilemma

"compunications"[34] and others simply the marriage of computers and telecommunications. Whereas the terms might appear different, the effects of the marriage are acknowledged to be astounding.

At the local level compunication has facilitated the transfer of data on university campuses, or in a city's dispersed departments, in dispersed corporation branches and in several other instances. At the national level scientific and business computer based information networks have been established. The Advanced Research Projects Agency (ARPANET), which is a government sponsored agency has used computer to computer communications for over twenty years. Using ARPANET researchers in universities and government research departments have exchanged information of research interest. Financial institutions use computer to computer communications to effect electronic fund transfers. One of the latest developments in office automation is electronic mail,[36] which will allow text to be transmitted regularly via computer to distant locations.

Communication media have changed remarkably. Traditionally telecommunications were via interconnected telephone wires, usually copper wires. Today links may be by cable, terrestrial microwave or satellites. The use of optical fiber cables has increased the amount of information and its accuracy as it is transmitted.

Another development which is affecting data transmission is the launching of terrestrial (space) communication satellites. Using a relay technique whereby signals are beamed to earth satellites, terrestrial satellites have served as interconnections for various earth stations. The first commercial transocean satellite INTELSAT I was launched in 1965 by the Communications Satellite Corporation (COMSAT) and owned by the International Telecommunications Satellite Consortium (INTELSAT). A series of INTELSAT satellites have been launched since to improve the quality of signals and performance. Presently Canadian, U.S. and European satellites have virtually crowded the skies over the Atlantic. Using these satellites, it is possible to send and receive messages to and from Europe and other parts of the world.

The American Telephone and Telegraph Company (AT&T) popularly known as "Ma Bell" had until recently monopolized voice and data communications. As a result of antitrust suits it was forced to share this role with other carriers. TELENET, MCI and later computer corporations like IBM will compete with AT&T in data communications. Some critics see an advantage and improvement in data communication since it will no longer be tied to Ma Bell's voice grade lines.

Cable television (CATV) is another medium which will affect data communications in the 1980s. Warner Communications Corporation has experimented with interactive CATV, with the toy name of "QUBE". While so far no tangible connections have been made with traditional information centers, the experiment might end up as a visible linkage between such centers and the home. Using CATV it might in the future be possible to access and search a computerized library catalog.

SOFTWARE TRENDS

Software is the term used to refer to programs which command a computer to perform specific functions. As Dolotta indicated, "without software, a general purpose computer is a useless collection of electronic and electromechanical components."[36] Four basic functions of the computer software may be identified. In the first place, there is the interface function—whereby software facilitates the interconnection of otherwise incompatible hardware. This is one of the most difficult aspects of the management of systems and centers, for even computers from the same manufacturer may not be able to "talk" to each other. Secondly, there is the access function which facilitates user machine interface. Thirdly, there is the multiple use facilitator function whereby simultaneously multiple users are allowed to use the same system. Finally, there is the programmers tool function whereby programmers are provided with editing devices usually referred to as utility programs.

Two broad categories of software may be isolated. The first are operating systems programs. These include system control programs (SCPs), utility programs, database management systems and communications control programs. Secondly, there are applications programs, written by programmers to perform specific functions.

In the hierarchy of significance, operating systems are the most crucial. An operating system (OS) is a set of programs designed to operate, manage and direct computer hardware. Different computer manufacturers provide different types of operating systems. Common terminology for IBM and IBM-compatible computers include TOS, OS, DOS, and VS which respectively stand for Tape Operating System, Operating System, Disk Operating System, and Virtual Storage Operating System. Other manufacturers may have different designations; for instance, Burroughs Corporation has MCP-Master Control Program as the equivalent of IBM's OS. As Table 1 indicates, sophisticated operating systems started with the third generation of computers in the 1960s.

Earlier generation computers were purchased as packages including software. In 1969, however, IBM the leader of the industry, started the policy of "unbundling"[37] of software—that is, sell it as a separate item. Consequently corporations specializing in developing of software have been established. The trends indicate that software will become more expensive than hardware mainly because it is extremely labor intensive.

CONCLUSION

Change in the information technological environment in which information professionals are operating today is extremely fast. Of prime importance calling for perpetual vigilance as we embrace this change is system reliability. Some people seem to have too much confidence in "that's what the computer says." Obviously computers are programmed by humans and in most cases computer output is a product of what a programmer or a group of programmers instructed them to perform. Most humans make mistakes some of the time. In other words, the old adage "garbage in garbage out" is too true to be dismissed as a system joke. What comes out of a computer system must thus be reexamined for validity sometimes based on simple subjective common sense.

We are living in a world with a high potential for developing inexpensive data processing power. What may be uneconomical today might be incredibly cheap within the near future. One of the greatest challenges of our time is how to define priorities using the technology around us and develop the appropriate software to implement such priorities. For information professionals it is imperative that they acquire the necessary computer literacy to be effective purveyors of information.

NOTES

1. Harry D. Huskey, "Computer Technology," *Annual Review of Information Science and Technology* 5 (1970):73.
2. James G. Williams, "Information Technology—A State of the Art,"

The Environment of Information Technology 41

Unpublished Paper Presented to the 1981 Pittsburgh Conference. The Challenge of Change—Critical Choices for Library Decision-Makers (November 2-4, 1981), p. 18.

3. Philip L. Long, "Computer Technology—An Update," *Annual Review of Information Science and Technology* 11 (1976):217.

4. Michael L. Dertouzos and Joel Moses, *The Computer Age: Twenty-Year View.* (Cambridge, Mass.: MIT Press, 1979), p. 321.

5. J. D. Lenk, *Handbook of Microprocessors, Microcomputers and Minicomputers.* (Englewood Cliffs, N.J.: Prentice-Hall, 1979), pp. 267-97.

6. Ronald D. Levine, "Supercomputers," *Scientific American* (January 1982): 118-135.

7. Huskey, "Computer Technology," p. 73.

8. Vennevar Bush, "As We May Think," *Atlantic Monthly* 176 (July 1945):101-8.

9. John C. Blair, "Micros, Minis and Mainframes... A Newcomers' Guide to the World of Computers—Especially Micros," *Online* 6 (January 1982):14-26.

10. Carver Mead and Lynn Conway, *Introduction to VLSI Systems.* (Reading, Mass.: Addison-Wesley 1980), Preface, p. vi.

11. Williams, "Information Technology," p. 2.

12. James Martin, *Telematic Society: A Challenge for Tomorrow.* (Englewood Cliffs, N.J.: Prentice-Hall, 1981), p. 3.

13. Edward K. Yasaki, "Tokyo Looks to the '90s," *Datamation* 28 (January 1982): 110-15.

14. Saul Rosen, "Electronic Computers: A Historical Survey," *Computing Surveys* 1 (March 1969):7-36.

15. William Davis and Allison McCormack, *The Information Age.* (Reading, Mass.: Addison-Wesley, 1979), pp. 67-70.

16. Norman Weizer, "A History of Operating Systems," *Datamation* 27 (January 1981):120, 122.

17. Martin O. Holoien, *Computers and Their Societal Impact.* (New York: Wiley 1977), pp. 44-47.

18. Dale F. Farmer, "IBM Compatible Giants," *Datamation* 27 (December 1981):94, 97.

19. Edward K. Yasaki, "Tokyo Looks," p. 110.

20. Mark D. Zimmerman, "Japan Throws Down the Computer Gauntlet," *Machine Design* 54 (February 1982):22, 24.

21. Frederic G. Withington, "Computer Technology: State of the Art," *Journal of the American Society for Information Science* 32 (March 1981):125.

22. Robert N. Noyce, "Hardware Prospects and Limitations," in Michael L. Dertouzos and Joel Moses, *The Computer Age: Twenty-Year View.* (Cambridge, Mass.: MIT Press, 1979), p. 333.

23. Frederick W. Miller, "Minis vs. Mainframes: Who's Doing Whose Job?" *Infosystems* 28 (May 1981):64.

24. Dale F. Farmer, "IBM-Compatible Giants," *Datamation* (December 1981):92-104.

25. Miller, "Minis vs. Mainframes," p. 68.

26. Carver Mead and Lynn Conway, *Introduction to VLSI Systems*. (Reading, Mass.: Addison-Wesley, 1980), Preface, p. v.

27. Alberto L. Sangiovanni-Vincentelli, IEEE Transactions on Circuits and Systems, *CAS* 28 (July 1981):617.

28. Author's interview with Automated Systems Office Staff of the Library of Congress, August 1981.

29. International Business Machines, *Introduction to IBM 3380 Direct Access Storage*. (White Plains, N.Y.: 1981):1.

30. James Martin, *Design of Man-Computer Dialogues*. (Englewood Cliffs, N.J.: Prentice-Hall, 1973), pp. 3-8.

31. Frederick W. Miller, "CRT Terminals Get Smarter, Cheaper," *Infosystems* 28 (September 1981):101-6.

32. Williams, "Information Technology," p. 114.

33. Martin, *Telematic Society*, Title page.

34. Manfred Kochen, "Technology and Communication in the Future," *Journal of the American Society for Information Science* 32 (March 1981):148.

35. Edward Morris, "Electronic Mail: Something for Everyone," *Infosystems* 23 (March 1981):54.

36. T. A. Dolotta, *Data Processing in 1980-1985* (New York: Wiley 1976), p. 87.

37. Alfred R. Berkeley, "Millionaire Machine," *Datamation* 27 (August 1981):34.

3
The Imperatives of Automation

Automation may have different connotations to different people. Professional literature indicates, however, that the concept of automation in the 1980s will be centered around the use of electronic equipment—particularly electronic digital computers. *Webster's New Collegiate Dictionary* defines automation as "the technique of making an apparatus, a process or a system operate automatically."[1] This implicitly connotes an entity which has a self-acting or self-regulating mechanism. In information processing, like any other automation endeavor, the procedure has four basic functional elements—input, process, output, and feedback. This closed-loop concept which is used in automated systems designs ensures product quality control. Figure 6 shows the main components of the closed-loop automation concept.

The computer as an aid to extending the capabilities of the human species has fascinated many a scientist. In the early 1970s, research in artificial intelligence resulted in the use of computers in performing societal functions which are normally done by human beings. Some scientists argued that because computers can think, remember and communicate, they are so similar to species of living beings to justify considering a symbiotic relationship between them and man. It was thus asserted that "man has acquired an important symbiote."[2] This intellectual euphoria and effervescent fascination with machine rationality exaggerated the extent to which artificial intelligence can be stretched.

Computers can indeed be said to think, remember and communicate. Nevertheless, they solely depend on anticipatory logic that has been built into them by the programmer. The programmer or a team of

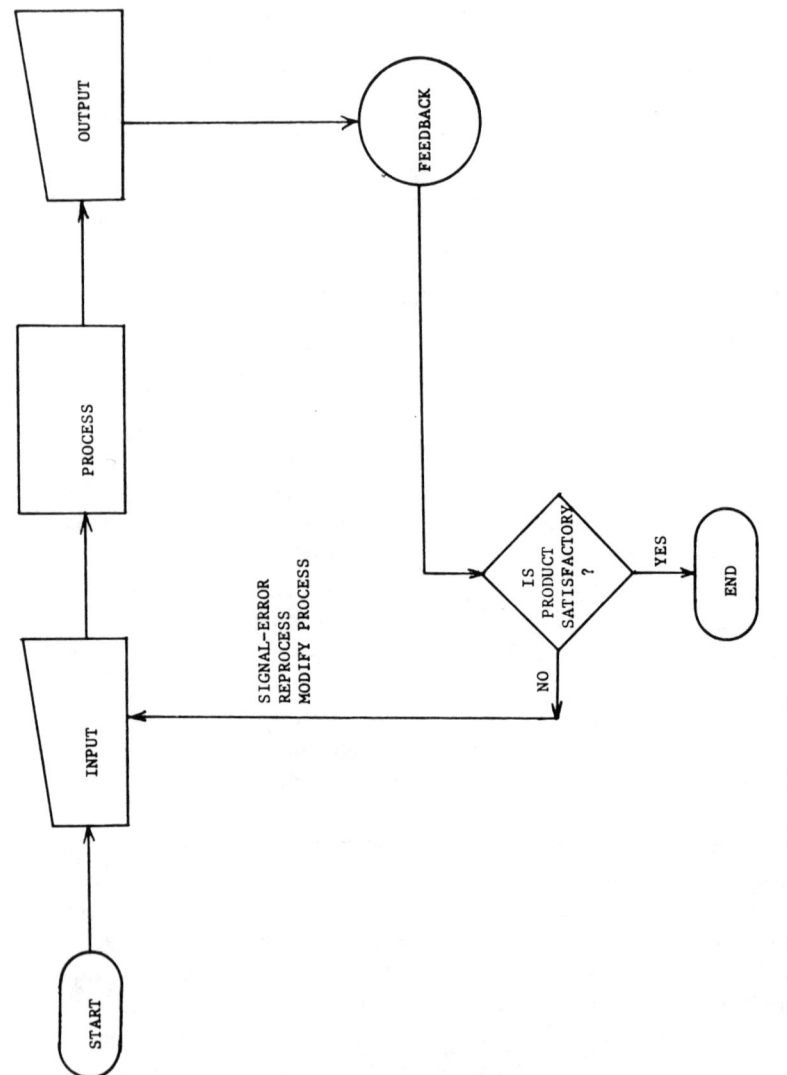

Figure 6. Automated Closed-Loop Concept

systems designers must either guess, calculate or otherwise predict all possible responses to a given problem or query. By the 1980s researchers had sobered up and realized the distinction between programmable and nonprogrammable human decisions or activities. Whereas the programmable activities are amenable to computerization, the nonprogrammable are very difficult to computerize. As Herbert Simon intimated, "the traditional methods for making nonprogrammed decisions in organizations—involving large amounts of human judgment, insight and intuition,"[3] are yet to be revolutionized. This observation is of utmost importance to information specialists, for while some enthusiasts have toyed with the concept of "total automation," empirical studies have shown that some aspects of information processing are very poor candidates for the automation enterprise. Such apparent skepticism by the author should not be misconstrued to mean an anti-automation stance. It rather reflects the need for caution in our excitement about automation.

Scanning the literature of information science one discerns signs of lack of awareness of progress of automation in the broader sense. Admittedly, automation of a factory, automation of an office, automation of a home and automation of information centers are essentially different. But they have a lot of common elements which can and should be explored and exploited. In order to avoid reinventing the wheel information scientists must be vigilant to developments in other sectors of automation. This calls for reading widely beyond the narrow confines of traditional professional literature.

Contrary to common beliefs, there are a lot of common denominators between information processing in business corporations and research libraries and information centers. Admittedly, there are differences too, but these should not be overemphasized at the expense of common aspects of processing. Four elements of information processing are illustrative of the commonality between information centers in corporations and research libraries. In the first place, stripped to the bare essentials, their rationale is similar. The rationale for seeking information for researchers, businessmen or the ordinary citizen has a very strong achievement motive. This motive is manifest in several different ways among information seekers. In the business environment, the predominant factor has historically been the maximization of profits while minimizing losses or costs. For researchers, the ultimate motive is for academic or scientific recognition. As regards the ordinary citizen self improvement has been supreme. Whatever term is used, whether research library, information center, management information system or simply library, the *raison d'etre* for the information facility is closely associated with the achievement motive of the information seeker.

Secondly, there is the element of urgency. Information seekers in especially industrialized countries have very short time spans between information need and information usage. Due to international business competition, speed at which information must be received has become critical. For instance, if an American corporation with a contract to supply minicomputers to a Venezuelan corporation cannot meet the deadline, Japanese or German computer corporations would fill the vacuum almost instantly. This urgency is equally important in the domestic market especially when the products are easily substitutable. For researchers, the earlier the projects are executed, the earlier the recognition. Similarly, for ordinary citizens, the earlier the information is received the earlier they achieve their self-improvement.

Thirdly, methodology has tended to be similar in that the electronic computer has been resorted to as the most appropriate tool to achieve the first two elements. Hitherto, it is the most efficient and fastest tool in information processing. This tendency to computerize has been accentuated by the volume of information needed by information seekers.

Finally, there is the universality of these concepts or elements of information processing. It is axiomatic that whether one is in Tokyo, Dakar, Buenos Aires, New York or London, the first three elements will be very significant for information providers.

How relevant is the foregoing discussion to automation? Early automation experiments in industry started with batch processing—whereby a task or group of tasks are submitted to be performed by the computer without continuous contact between computer and human operator. Processing advanced to a stage where jobs could be submitted interactively—with the human operator directing the computer operation as he saw fit. Presently, one of the most researched aspects is the use of a common database which can be accessible to all eligible operators. The use of a common database introduced the database management system concept (DBMS) which was discussed in Chapter 2.

Information centers have gone through similar steps in automation progress, but always lagging behind industry in the new applications. In order to avoid this lag, some of the large research libraries and information centers could initiate research projects in computer applications. While it is realized that some have already embarked on such projects, for instance at the University of Illinois, Stanford University, MIT, and New York Public Library, more research effort could be initiated by large research libraries.

In addition, information scientists working in research libraries should be prepared to adapt, adopt or experiment with concepts which have been developed in the business environment. During the 1980s, libraries and information centers will see more computers than ever before. Concepts like database management systems, data communications and teleconferencing are being perfected in industry. Very few libraries or information centers have constructively thought of how these new technologies could be utilized in library functions. What is urgently needed is a reexamination of the incentives for automation and a re-tailoring of automation projects to achieve desirable objectives.

INCENTIVES FOR AUTOMATION

Four fundamental incentives have been identified in either industry, business or in information centers thus:

1. *Cost Reduction*—staff services, operational costs and overhead expenses
2. *Service Improvement*—through reliability, accuracy, and promptness
3. *Performance/Effectiveness Control*—through regular checks
4. *The Bandwagon*—appearing to be abreast of current practices

In an extensive study of the computer revolution in British industries, Stoneman[4] emphasized the first three. Conventional wisdom in information science literature likewise agrees that these have been important motive forces to automate. The pros and cons of incentives 1 to 3 have been abundantly analyzed in literature. While the fourth has often been glossed over, it is perhaps one of the most influential factors in giving automation a bad name.

It seems to be human nature for individuals and the institutions they control to strive to be part of the *avant-garde*. After all, that is how esteem is acquired. In the automation enterprise, however, the price to pay for jumping on the bandwagon has in some cases been very high. The bandwagon phenomenon has been prevalent both in business and in libraries. As Diebold indicated,

There is no point in automation at all simply for the sake of automating. It is a rare executive who will admit that his company is investigating this field simply because his golf partner's company has already installed equipment or because he has been overwhelmed by glamorous advertisements and newspaper stories. Nonetheless, there are reasons to believe that at least as many supposedly hard-headed businessmen have bought expensive equipment on this basis.[5]

Libraries and information centers had similar reactions to automation from the 1960s through the 1970s. Commenting on the introduction of OCLC (Online Computer Library Center) in 1968, DeGennaro indicated how the "glamour and value of being 'online' was irresistible."[6] This was certainly an archtypal case of "being with it."

Five negative influences have been mainly due to the bandwagon syndrome. In the first place, poorly planned local information systems have been implemented. Some such systems have sprouted without basic strategic planning questions like—is it necessary to automate this function? Is it cost effective? What are the short and long range effects on our current operations? And perhaps most important, do we have trained personnel to operate the function or system as introduced? Management at the critical decision level has in most cases not asked the right questions before a new system or function is introduced.

Secondly, poorly designed local, regional or national information networks based on automation principles have been established. Even when they appear to have been established with foresight some services of national networks sometimes malfunction because of overload due to "bandwagon riders." One of the complaints about the OCLC as compared to RLIN (Research Libraries Information Network) or WLN (Washington Library Network) has been the quality of records in the master database. This defect may be traceable to the bandwagon effect.

Thirdly, there has been a lot of frustration on the part of information seekers. The 1960s and 1970s were characterized by higher failure rates of information systems. In several cases computers billed customers who had never used or ceased to use the services claimed. While this may be a human rather than a system error, it has been a consequence of staff who are ill equipped to operate the newly implemented system.

The fourth influence is the elephantine problem of the interconnection of local, regional or national future information systems. Systems designers (who in the 1980s include several for library systems) face insurmountable problems. Some of the systems they have to remodify or redesign were implemented at such a rush that coordinating the existing subsystems is extremely difficult. At the national level, computer based library networks have sprung up on the U.S. scene in the last decade or so. But as Markuson indicated, "a critical issue we must face is that present systems and organizations are ad hoc developments."[7]

Finally, the bandwagon syndrome may be responsible for retardation of automation projects. Some of the mistakes resulting from poorly planned systems have slowed down development projects. In spite of its giant success some aspects of OCLC which were ill-conceived resulted in the withdrawal of a number of research institutions to join RLIN.

INFORMATION CENTERS AND LIBRARIES

The definitions of information centers and libraries are dynamic variants of very similar information processing entities. The subtle difference lies in the functional emphasis of each institution. An information center usually emphasizes provision of information and minimal documents. On-line data banks may be cited as examples of information centers. BRS (Bibliographical Retrieval Services), SDC (Systems Development Corporation) and Lockheed Information Retrieval Systems normally provide information about available citations rather than documents. On the other hand, the conventional library provides more documents than information. It must be pointed out that this distinction may in some cases be blurred in individual institutions.

Information centers have been developed beyond providing citations to providing summaries of the citations. Many information centers which were commercially developed to sell bibliographical information became computerized. In case of on-line data banks, the question of whether or not to automate is irrelevant. However, when the term is extended to include abstracting and indexing services like Chemical Abstracts, Engineering Index and National Library of Medicine's MEDLARS (Medical Literature Analysis Retrieval System) the general incentive for automation applies.

As regards libraries of all types the most significant incentives to automate have been the dual decrease in fiscal support and increasing demands of the services they offer. These library woes are adequately discussed in library literature. Library administrators have for the last decade or so attempted to use computers in automating traditional functions. In the mid-seventies, the definition of library automation was given in one of the leading information science publications as "application of the computer to routine operations and services."[8] The Information Age will certainly affect the traditional functions of libraries as they compete with aggressive commercially organized information providers. As Wilfred Lancaster[9] aptly indicated, the library of the future will not merely be a cosmetically different institution from the present library. It is most likely that in a predominantly paperless information era the library will have to change both its contents and mode of operation. As will be discussed in the rest of this text, of all information providing institutions, the library will face some of the strongest challenges to its existence during the Information Age. There are several indications to exemplify these challenges.

In the first instance, there is a tremendous increase in the number of information professionals who are non-librarians. In a study sponsored by the National Science Foundation, published in 1981, it was found that librarians form only 10% of the aggregate pool of information professionals.[10] Although the study was not a longitudinal measurement over a long period, the research team agreed that there has been a gradual decrease of the librarians' percentage in the last two to three decades.

Secondly, new technologies for information storage and retrieval as discussed in Chapter 2 will progressively make what Maurice Line[11] called POP (print-on-paper) obsolete or relatively rarely used. Lancaster[12] has convincingly argued that future scientists will be able to communicate to each other and conduct normal research in a paperless mode, using the computer terminal as the main tool. With the medley of information technologies increasing almost daily, one tends to agree with Tom Suprenant that "never before has the entire host of technologies combined not only to challenge the role of the library, but at the same time."[13]

Finally, there is the challenge of information entrepreneurs variously known as information brokers, information jobbers or simply information vendors. Prior to the on-line revolution in information processing, libraries were virtually unchallenged in the public sector as providers of information. As will be discussed in Chapter 4, middlemen took away many of the services traditionally provided by libraries. Using business methods, some of the most effective have had lucrative contracts from business corporations and the U.S. federal government.

Throughout history, the library has provided information to the business sector, academic institutions, government, and the public at large. This role is slipping away largely because libraries have been very slow in responding to the changing environment. At this juncture, a number of pertinent questions will highlight the issues at hand. Are libraries and information centers gearing to the demands of the Information Age? Are library planners prepared to use modern business concepts like strategic planning which marshals available capital, targeted market, financial resources, human resources and institutional goals to effectively achieve desired objectives? Are information specialists constantly monitoring developments in the information technology to effect congenial adoptions for library applications? The dynamic information professionals are making a lot of progress. According to Lancaster, "The [library] profession seems to have its head in the sand."[14] In the meantime the clock moves on and the onslaught of the Information Age races like a raging fire. Unless librarians reexamine their *raison d'etre* and *modus operandi*, they will find themselves stranded along the path to a paperless society, as custodians of the dinosaurs of the Information Age. The time for a thorough reevaluation is definitely now for tomorrow will be a post Information Age.

CORPORATION INFORMATION SYSTEMS

Largely due to availability of capital financing for development, information systems in business have a higher potential for automation. Nevertheless, other than some of the large corporations which have combined data processing, administrative systems, and marketing information systems, many corporations are beginning the process of restructuring the information gathering and disseminating function. Traditionally, two subsystems may be identified, the manufacturing oriented subsystem and the management subsystem.

In manufacturing industries, computer assisted design (CAD) and computer assisted manufacturing (CAM) are likely to dominate factory activities in the 1980s. As computers become smaller, more powerful and less costly, there will be a trickle down effect in computer use from larger manufacturing enterprises to smaller ones. Currently, the automobile and aeronautical industries are among the major users of these technologies.

Computer assisted design relies heavily on computer graphics and mass storage concepts. Product designs are recorded on disk in digital form and retrieved for screen (CRT) display whenever required. Using an electronically sensitive light pen, modifications can be made on the design of say an airplane or an automobile. Although most corporations are still experimenting with CAD, some engineers have claimed realization of practical benefits. At McDonne Aircraft Company, St. Louis, King[15] claimed that CAD has led to: increased productivity, better management control, greater design freedom, shorter lead time, improved reliability and reduced maintenance.

Computer assisted manufacturing is a very close adjunct of CAD. Manufacturing operations are predesigned, and stored in computer memory. Using computer controlled switching systems, operations are activated and machines are instructed to function as required. In the 1980s, CAM will be a major feature of manufacturing with computer controlled robots performing many of the functions.

There has been a multitude of reactions to CAD/CAM experiments. Herbert Simon simply dismisses those trends as "natural continuation of the industrial revolution."[16] On the other hand, Kenneth Klee suggests that they presage the "second industrial revolution."[17] Whether we visualize it as evolutionary or revolutionary, the advent of the so-called "factory of the future," which is in effect the factory of the 1980s, will have a dramatic effect on information resource centers for design engineers. In a push button factory, which is computer operated, the design engineers will certainly get most of their information in digital form rather than in hard-paper form from a traditional technical library.

With regard to management information systems, the 1980s are putting data processing departments in disarray. Data processing managers not only have to redefine their roles in their parent corporations, but they have to reexamine their relationship with the information users they serve. Traditionally, the information gathering and dissemination function in the American corporation was dispersed in several service points. The production division would have the materials inventory information system; the marketing division would have the marketing information system; the finance division would have the accounting system; the general administration division would have the general information system; and the corporation library would provide all the residual information it could muster. In the traditional structural arrangement, the data processing department was no more than a facility to service the functional departments of the organization.

The corporation of the Information Age has to undergo a metamorphosis imposed by external forces. For one thing the once secure markets are no longer sacrosanct. Thus most corporations have had to expand beyond the domestic market in order to survive. The invasion of the U.S. domestic market and the international market by Japanese industrialists makes U.S. corporations very vulnerable. International competition has been accentuated by the advent of the so called "new Japans"—Korea, Hong Kong, and Taiwan, which are flooding markets with industrial products. Realizing these new trends, some critics have pointed to the lack of preparation thus: "Currently, we sell in world markets. Our industrial competition is global in nature. But as a society, we lack the image of ourselves as a global competitor, and the constrained view is reflected in declining industrial institutions."[18]

Corporations which attempt to get out of the stalemate visualize automation as the ultimate salvage and thus enters management information system (MIS). Using the MIS concept, corporations have attempted to cluster the information gathering and dissemination functions under one umbrella. Such a strategy puts a firm grip on one of the most important resources—information. Garvin[19] and Poppel[20] have convincingly argued that during the Information Age, corporations which mismanage their information function will be losers and may be squeezed out of existence.

Whereas there appears to be no universally accepted definition of what is an MIS, practitioners seem to agree that its basic function is to provide management with relevant information. Mitchel Salmere cited one of the most precise prescriptions for an MIS by saying that the function of an ideal MIS should be producing "exactly enough of the most relevant information at precisely the right moment to produce an infallible management decision and at the least possible cost."[21] An effective MIS has thus to move from the traditional mode of operation whereby the data processing department was simply a processing service facility. It has to do more analysis and sieving information for top management than ever before, so that the prime decision makers are screened from the chaff information. As Horton commented "Nobody said the job was going to be easy; it isn't."[22]

This integrated analytical approach to corporate information processing has far-reaching implications. In the first place, MIS personnel must have a firm grasp of the corporations' objectives and marshal its efforts to the execution of those objectives. Secondly, there must be a centralization of the information function. While this does not necessarily mean that all components must be under the same roof, top decisions concerning the function must emanate from the same source. Thirdly, MIS personnel ought to learn to communicate in language other than pure technical jargon. At critical moments, top management has too little time to learn new acronyms, some of which may be obsolete the following day. Fourthly, there must be regular appraisal of MIS department by its head to ascertain that company objectives are met. Fifthly, in order to be effective, the head of MIS must be among the top executives, to get first-hand information about major decisions so that critical functional information can be given its due priority. As a rule of thumb, the head of MIS ought to report directly to the president and chief executive of the corporation. Finally, it is desirable that the chief of MIS has a profound knowledge of both information systems and business operations. Such knowledge may be acquired through formal education or long experience.

MIS is thus an automation pregnant concept whose implementation is manifest in the reorganization of the corporation information function. With the current trends towards paperless information systems, the traditional components like corporation libraries or data processing units may have to play new roles. In some instances, it might be more cost effective to bypass these units and purchase information products from commercial information vending houses.

COMPUTER BASED RESOURCE SHARING NETWORKS

As a practical expediency, resource sharing covers the whole gamut of automation programs. The concept "resource sharing" connotes the pooling of goods and services which may be utilized by entities which subscribe to the existence of the pool. It is not limited to non-profit, not-for-profit or government sponsored pools. In a purely commercial environment like banking, insurance or transportation resources are shared at a price fixed by the resource controller.

With regard to networking, the term "network" refers to an assemblage of components with the purpose of achieving specific goals and objectives. Whereas there are several types of networks (for instance the telephone network, the electric power and lighting network and water supply network), an information network is set up to store and transmit information. In the 1980s, most of the major information networks will be computer based. Various types of network configurations are discussed in professional literature. With the current trends in hardware and data communication systems, the most common architectures will be the distributed centralized network and the decentralized star network as shown in Figure 7. The former (7a) will have a central high powered processing facility, while the latter architecture will not.

Information networks may be local, regional or national. With the use of satellite communications, we now have international information networks. An ideal computer based information network has four basic elements. In the first place, it must have digitized data or information to communicate from one node to another. Secondly, it must have large scale storage devices to facilitate the storage of the pool of information to be used. Thirdly, it must have an elaborate automatic switching system to direct data to the appropriate node. Finally, it must have a data distribution system to the end nodes where the ultimate user will utilize the information transmitted.

Why computer-based resource sharing networks? Some of the salient factors for an increase and constant use of networks include:

1. *Availability of Appropriate Technology*—due to VLSI, mini and microcomputers will be on the market, at reasonable prices, to perform the sophisticated switching mechanisms.
2. *Economies of Scale*—will be realized through increased use of automated devices in homes, offices and information centers.
3. *Efficiency*—in data communication will be achieved when networks are shared. This would result from the reduction of "idle time" in the data communication system.
4. *Competition*—among information providers or their clients will accentuate the need for shared networks to speed up data communications.
5. *Aggressive Business Practices*—of network systems designers and vendors. Several corporations are developing data communications network packages. Among the best known are: Xerox's ETHERNET, Wang Laboratories WANGNET, IBM's SNA. Persuasive marketing will induce information managers into buying or leasing local networks.

a. Distributed Centralized Network

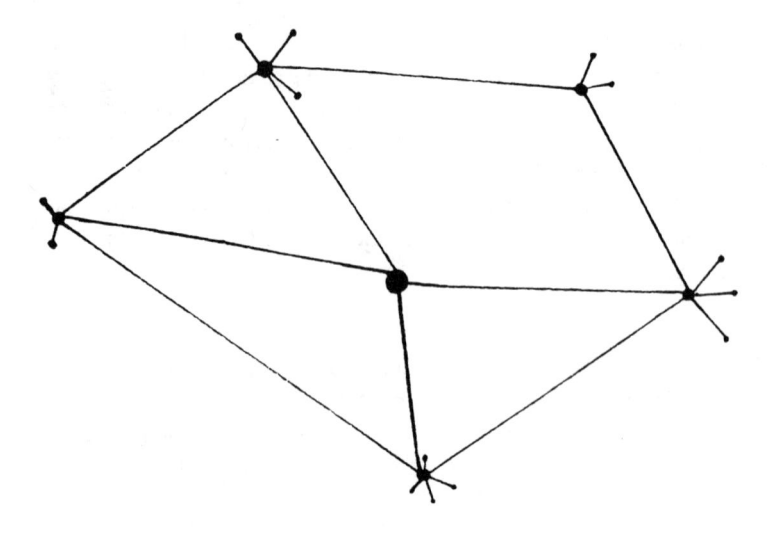

b. Centralized Star Network

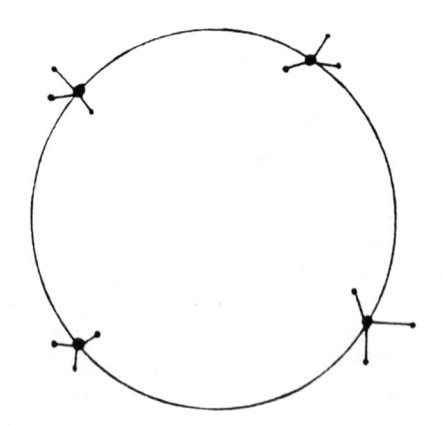

Figure 7. Network Architecture

OFFICE AUTOMATION

The early 1980s will go down in history as the period when the term "office of the future" was no more than a buzz term. Stepping into the information age inevitably implies defining the new modes of information handling. Office automation is such a mode which is comprehensive and has several components. Definitions of office automation abound in information science literature. Saffady's definition is one of the most expressive, for he defined office automation as "the application of technology to the creation, storage, manipulation, retrieval, reproduction, and dissemination of information in an office environment."[23] In strategic planning for office automation, however, such a definition must be broadened to include careful integration of human resources. As Rockhold[24] asserted, the best technological arrangement will collapse if the people involved are not blended into the planning scheme.

Definitions aside, the technological base for office automation relies heavily on computer based networking.[25] The much publicized networks like ETHERNET developed by Xerox Corporation, SNA (System Network Architecture) by IBM, ARCNET by Datapoint and WANGNET by Wang Laboratories are network designs to facilitate communication of data among system components. These local networks—usually referred to as CBXs (Computer Based Exchange) are equivalent to the Bell System PBX (Private Branch Exchange). They may either be shared by corporations or dedicated to one corporation.

By wiring managers together electronically, office automation is certainly the ultimate in corporate information systems. Indications are that productivity will be enhanced when busy executives use teleconferencing instead of long distance travel[26] or call up data from electronic publishers to illustrate a point, or use graphic terminals to demonstrate to the board market behavior in the last 24 hours. Scanning relevant literature reveals eight major elements of office automation:

1. Word Processing
2. Electronic Mail
3. Teleconferencing
4. Facsimile Transmission
5. Computer Graphics
6. Executive Desktop Terminals
7. Microcomputers
8. Personnel Training and Adjustment

All the elements with the possible exception of the last one have been discussed in depth in professional literature. The list is certainly not exhaustive for a number of other elements could be added. The first five are essentially technologies, whereas the last three may be classified as facilitators of the technologies. The treatment which we give these technologies and the facilitators is the same that pervades the whole of the text. In an office environment, technologies are no more than tools to help the critical decision maker in an organization make an optimum decision in the shortest possible time. Thus the detailed description of the functioning of the technologies is left to other texts. Our concern is the relative importance of these technologies.

Given an appropriate environment, word processing permits easy manipulation (edit, add, delete, etc.) of textual information. This process takes a lot of time of the clerical personnel. Some studies have shown that management spends 5-10% of office time waiting for information to be processed. With word processing systems this portion of wasted time will be reduced. Electronic mail as a technology, allows the digital transmission of messages between offices. Messages may be displayed on CRT screens or printed out on paper terminals. The concept of teleconferencing on the other hand, implies a visual transmission of both voice and the images of the people communicating. This may be at short or long distances. The last two, facsimile transmission and computer graphics, are equally important in office automation. Facsimile transmission (FAX) entails transmission of the text virtually verbatim, whereas computer graphics demonstrates charts, graphs or tables in multicolored formats.

The last three elements facilitating office automation have been partly discussed in Chapter 2. To provide each executive with a desktop terminal allows him to access whatever data has been programmed into a central data bank. This may be in turn facilitated by a built in microcomputer or microprocessor in the desktop terminal. Finally, personnel training and adjustment is perhaps one of the most important aspects of office automation. In several cases automation programs have failed because of poor initiation of office personnel into the automation program.

Productivity might eventually be enhanced by office automation. As Frederic Withington[27] has indicated, however, it is not usually possible to know ahead of time how effective the new systems will be. What seems to be certain is that the corporation information base, information processing and dissemination will be markedly changed.

HOME AUTOMATION

Commercial and academic research organizations have produced an impressive list of services[28] which home consumers are likely to purchase during the Information Age. Three broad categories of such services may be identified, the entertainment services, the educational services and the functional services. A selection from the commonly quoted services runs as follows:

1. *Entertainment Services*
   Computer games—Star Wars, Chess, Ping Pong, Pac-Man
   Local and national entertainment guides
   Sports information updates
   Computerized dating services
   Restaurant and hotel guides
2. *Educational Services*
   Computer assisted learning packages
   Interactive public discussions
   Medical and hygiene public services
   Local information sources—city guides
   Publications services—where to find what?
3. *Functional Services*
   Electronic purchase and fund transfer
   Banking services
   Remote control of domestic appliances—air conditioning, oven operation
   Weather reports and forecasts
   Touring and holiday guides
   Working at home—office interconnections
   Information databanks searching
   Emergency services—police, paramedic, fire
   Travel reservations—air, bus, boat

Comprehensive home automation presupposes four developmental requirements as either given or concomitant. In the first place, there must be central large-scale storage centers operated on a commercial basis, by public utilities or by government institutions. Such centers would serve as sources for most of the information used in the home. Secondly, there must be computer based efficient switching networks to facilitate data transfer. Thirdly, there must be effective data communications systems for massive data to be transmitted. This may call for extensive use of optical fiber technology, which is an improvement over the copper wire transmission used for the conventional telephone lines. Finally, there must be mass produced easily accessible computer program packages for stand alone operations.

Most of these requirements will take a considerable amount of time to develop. As Joel Moses[29] and many other analysts have indicated home automation will not arrive all at once. While some of the applications will be implemented within the next few years, others will be gradually evolutionary. What seems certain is that the home automation process will increase the tempo of production and sale of information products and services.

SYSTEM RELIABILITY, BACKUPS AND SECURITY

One of the most devastating accidents during the Information Age will be the automated information systems "crash." System failures may be attributed to the malfunctioning of hardware components, software errors or human errors. Experienced system designers incorporate safeguards in the designs to account for such accidents. In the designer's language, built in checks ensure that systems "failsafe" and cause minimal interruption of the flow of the data processing function of the organization. Three critical measures are used to appraise system reliability. First there is the Mean Time Between Failures (MTBF)—how long does the system run before a failure occurs. Second, there is the Mean Time To Repair (MTTR)—how soon can the system be repaired and put back to normal operation. Finally, there is the recovery rate—given 100 percent data in the system, how much of that data can be recovered in case of an accident.

The importance of the magnitude of these measures may differ in different data processing environments. It must be pointed out, however, that in the 1980s, most people will be accustomed to using automated systems. Thus the ability to minimize or control system failures will spell information managers' success or disdain.

Backup subsystems are used extensively to remedy complete loss of vital data. To ensure continuous flow of processing, some organizations use two parallel systems so that one may continue when the alternate system malfunctions. As regards specific jobs, backup files are created and stored on secure subsystems (tapes or disks) during processing. When a crash occurs, these backups are reactivated and files recreated.

As discussed in Chapter 1, security of especially personal data will be a major issue in the Information Age. The proliferation of information networks, locally, nationally and internationally, into which subscribers will plug will accentuate the problem. As is usually the case, cheap nets will be more amenable to security problems than the more expensive ones.

CONCLUSION

The imperatives of automation will magnify the diversity of computer based information systems in the 1980s. Business survival, office reorganization for productivity, and domestic convenience will all be pegged to these systems. As we get deeper into the Information Age, information products and services will be touted, marketed and bought in increasing numbers. Some of the basic questions we may ask as participants include: Are these products reliable? Do they have built in security devices to protect clients' privacy? What if the system crashes? While the lure for automation will be higher, the price we may have to pay may include a surrender (however limited) of personal privacy.

NOTES

1. *Webster's New Collegiate Dictionary, 8th Edition* (Springfield, Mass.: G. & C. Merriam Company, 1976).

2. John G. Kemeney, *Man and the Computer* (New York: Scribner's, 1972), p. 13.

3. Herbert Simon, *The New Science of Management Decision* (Englewood Cliffs, N.J.: Prentice Hall, 1979), pp. 39-81.

4. Paul Stoneman, *Technological Diffusion and the Computer Revolution: The UK Experience* (Cambridge, England: Cambridge University Press, 1976), pp. 160-90.

5. John Diebold, *Beyond Automation, Managerial Problems of an Expanding Technology* (New York: Praeger, 1970), p. 70.

6. Richard DeGennaro, "Research Libraries Enter the Information Age," *Library Journal* 104 (November 15, 1979):2408.

7. Barbara E. Markuson, "Revolution and Evolution: Critical Issues in Library Network Developments," in Barbara E. Markuson, *Networks for Networkers* (New York: Neal-Schuman Publishers, 1980), pp. 12-13.

8. Audrey N. Grosch, "Library Automation," *Annual Review of Information Science and Technology* 11 (1976):225.

9. Wilfred F. Lancaster, "Whither Libraries? or Wither Libraries," *College and Research Libraries* 39 (September 1978):345.

10. Anthony Debons, et al., *The Information Professional* (New York: Marcel Dekker 1981), p. 2.

11. Maurice B. Line, "Libraries and Information Services in a Post-Technology Society." *Journal of Library Automation* 14 (December 1981):258.

12. Lancaster, "Whither Libraries?" pp. 351-56.

13. Tom Suprenant, "Future Libraries: The Electronic Environment," *Wilson Library Bulletin* 56 (January 1982):340. Revised by author.

14. Lancaster, "Whither Libraries?" p. 357.

15. Hulas H. King, "A Total Integrated Approach to CAD/CAM." In *CAD/CAM VII 1979: Detroit Michigan* (Detroit: American Society of Mechanical Engineers, 1979): Section 2.

16. Simon, *The New Science*, p. 19.

17. Kenneth Klee, "CAD/CAM: Who's in Charge," *Datamation* 28 (February 1982):110.

18. Thomas G. Gunn, *Computer Applications in Manufacturing* (New York: Industrial Press 1981), p. 182.

19. Andrew P. Garvin, *How to Win With Information or Lose Without It* (Washington, D.C.: Bermont Books 1980), pp. 16-17.

20. Harvey L. Poppel, "The Information Revolution: Winners and Losers," *Harvard Business Review* 56 (January-February 1978):159.

21. Mitchel B. Salmere, "How to Improve a Management Information System," *Infosystems* 28 (November 1981):90.

22. Forest Woody Horton, Jr., "Information Management Czardom or Stardom?" *Information and Records Management* 15 (July 1981):50.

23. William Saffady, *Automated Office: An Introduction to the Technology* (Silver Spring, Md.: National Micrographics Association, 1981), p. 1.

24. Alan G. Rockhold, "Keys to Successful Office Automation: Company Strategies and User Needs," *Infosystems* 29 (March 1982):66.

25. Kenneth Klee, et al. "Battle of the Networks," *Datamation* 28 (March 1982):127.

26. Andrew Pollack, "Automated Office to Give Managers a Competitive Edge," *New York Times* (Sunday, January 10, 1982): Section 12, p. 38.

27. Frederic G. Withington, "Coping with Computer Proliferation," *Harvard Business Review* 58 (May-June 1980):152-53.

28. James Martin, *Telematic Society: A Challenge for Tomorrow* (Englewood Cliffs, N.J.: Prentice-Hall, 1981), pp. 121-138.

29. Joel Moses, "The Computer in the Home," in Michael L. Dertouzos and Joel Moses, *The Computer Age: A Twenty Year View* (Cambridge, Mass.: MIT Press, 1979), pp. 3-20.

4
The Information Industry and Market in the United States

In this chapter, we attempt to make an analytical survey of two symbiotically poised components of the information infrastructure. The information industry and market are essentially the production and distribution elements of the information activity. The imperatives to automate discussed in Chapter 3 are partly a function of the availability of hardware and software products. It should also be recognized that the urge to automate may be heightened by marketing hypes, persuasion, and sometimes deception by the market operators. Thus analysis of the industry and market broadens the scope in which the information dilemma will be visualized. On the other hand, the problems of user access discussed in Chapter 5 are highlighted by what manufacturers decide to produce. Likewise, access may be limited by what marketing agencies decide to put on the market.

Chapter 4, therefore, has a bridge function connecting two of the concepts developed in the text. First, the decision to automate depends, to a large extent, on what is produced. Second, user accessibility to information depends on what material is available "out there." As to whether the material available satisfies user needs will be discussed in the following chapter.

One of the most comprehensive analyses of the information activity vis-à-vis the national economy was reported in a study made by the U.S. Department of Commerce.[1] This nine volume study attempted to define the activity and prescribe measurement parameters. Analysis of the primary and secondary sectors includes both automated and manual elements. In our approach, however, we emphasize the information industry and market based on electronic devices. We stress the role of the computer and its peripherals or accessories in information transfer.

Due to its vast natural resources, the United States has for a long time played a leading role in high technology industries. Information technology is one of the sectors of society where this supremacy has been manifest. Foreign scholars[2] and statesmen[3] have often acknowledged this supremacy. At the national level, the 1980s are witnessing a high correlation between high technology and economic power. As Frohman stipulated: "No one doubts any more that to be more competitive with foreign companies U.S. manufacturers need to increase their investment in R&D. Indeed, technology can be a powerful weapon on the battlefield of economic enterprise."[4] At the corporation level, some of the progressive corporation's Chief Executive Officers (CEOs) are using high level information technology to track down competitors' business performance.[5] In other words, in the 1980s, diligent use of technology will predicate economic performance at the national level and business success at the corporation level. While technology *per se* may not be the panacea for low productivity, it will certainly be a significant element for economic success in the 1980s decade.

Why discuss the U.S. information industry and market? Why not Japan or Germany or Canada? Other than convenience and ready access to relevant documentation, the U.S. scene is one of the most dynamic and developed. Discussing the U.S. scenario thus gives us a microcosm of the global picture within the 1980s context. This is with a proviso that we recognize that high information technology is a phenomenon of industrialized societies. Inevitably what is discussed in this chapter will most likely preclude many of the so-called Third World countries.

Whereas it is plausible to assert that "U.S. manufacturers have had the world's computer market largely to themselves,"[6] sustained preeminence will require careful strategic planning and investment in research and development. Some industry analysts have demonstrated that the U.S. has for some time lagged behind other industralized countries. According to Leopold Froehlich,[7] U.S. productivity increased only 1.1% between 1967-77. In contrast, Japan had 6.2%, West Germany 4.2%, Italy 3.6% and United Kingdom 2.4%. While these figures exclude farming, they include all other elements of the industrial sector. Some analysts have argued that with the use of artificial intelligence there may be an upturn in U.S. performance. "With the aid of robots—so goes the consensus—productivity will increase and U.S. industry will be made whole again."[8] This is a *prima facie* judgment, for robots have yet to prove their cost-effectiveness.

THE INFORMATION INDUSTRY

We are cognizant of the several definitions of information or industry and connotations attached to them. For the purposes of this text, we shall adopt Alan Gilpin's definition of industry. He clarified that, "Specifically, an industry comprises all those activities which are directed to the production of a given class of goods, e.g. aircraft, ships, machine tools, foodstuffs etc.... An individual firm may make a wide range of dissimilar goods."[9] This definition will be expanded to accommodate two interrelated connotations of the information industry. The first is a consideration of information manipulation equipment—especially the electronic digital computers. Second, we shall consider information generation and processing services—especially on-line database production.

In its purest form, information is an intangible good, for information is that which is communicated to be understood. Ultimately, the individual researcher, thinker, or inventor is the prime producer of information. Due to modern technology and the demands of the present society, however, the product as received by the end user goes through several stages of processing. Consequently, such a product makes the inventor's piece basically a raw material. Figure 8 is a simplified model of information utilization. The enclosed circles indicate the multitude of components at each of the four stages of production and utilization. While the information industry (hardware, software, and services) is not specifically mentioned in the cycle, it is the main facilitator of stage II.

Within such a conceptual framework, two broad categories may be identified in the information industry. First, the public sector, which is composed of publicly funded agencies. Inevitably, the federal government dominates this sector. Through its various agencies like the National Aeronautical and Space Administration (NASA), the Department of Health and Human Services (formerly HEW) and the Department of Defense (DOD) it produces and processes masses of information. In addition, there are state agencies and independent not-for-profit institutions.

Second, there is the very variegated private sector. This may be

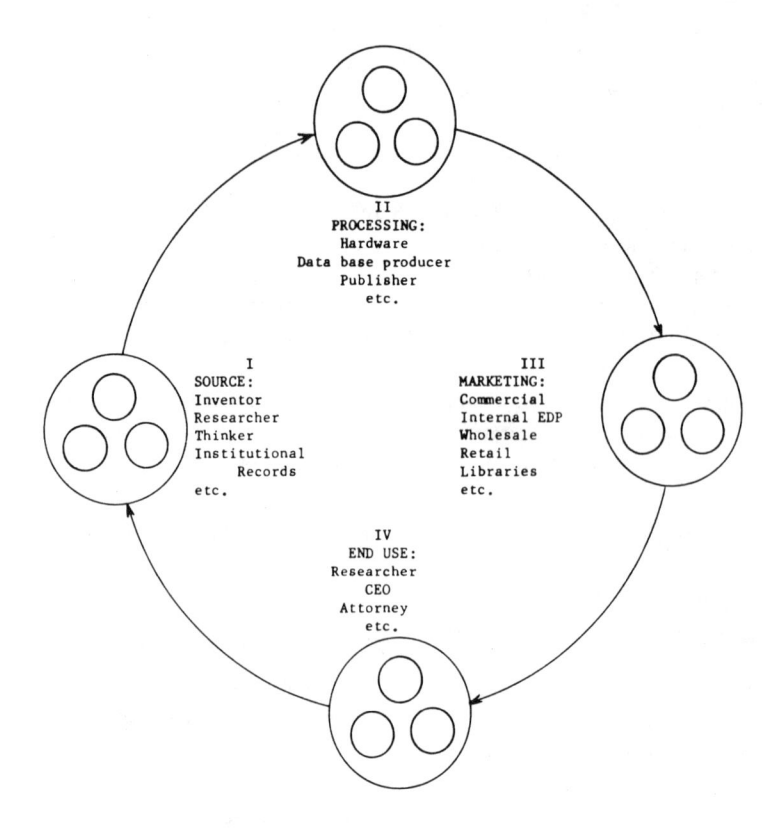

```
                    II
                PROCESSING:
                 Hardware
            Data base producer
                 Publisher
                   etc.

    I                              III
  SOURCE:                       MARKETING:
  Inventor                      Commercial
  Researcher                    Internal EDP
  Thinker                       Wholesale
  Institutional                 Retail
         Records                Libraries
  etc.                          etc.

                   IV
                END USE:
                Researcher
                   CEO
                 Attorney
                   etc.
```

Figure 8. Information Utilization Cycle

subdivided into: information hardware producers, information software producers, data communication channels producers, on-line databases, and producers of reprographic materials.

The Dynamics of the Hardware Industry

Understanding the hardware industry is invaluable to our perception of the information infrastructure. Three main types of computers are currently being manufactured, namely, the mainframes, minicomputers, and micro (desk top) computers. Professional literature has often referred to mainframes as elephants and micros as rabbits. By the same token, perhaps it is not too farfetched to refer to minis as horses!

In 1980, *Datamation* magazine instituted an annual survey of the top 100 computer manufacturing companies in the United States. This analysis is somewhat analogous to the *Fortune* 500, which lists the largest U.S. corporations. The survey gives a good indication of major fluctuations in the computer industry. Likewise, *Standard and Poor's Industry Surveys* do give comprehensive analyses of the industry on an annual basis. Yet another source of trend information is the Annual National Computer Conference report summarized in the *Computer World*.

Some general observations can be made about the trends in the computer industry. In the first place, computer hardware is becoming increasingly cheaper to buy or rent. As it happens, users are currently getting more units of computing power per dollar than say ten years ago. Consequently, people or institutions which had hitherto never thought of acquiring computers are becoming part of an enlarged user group.

Secondly, computer hardware is becoming more versatile. As partly discussed in Chapter 3, computer usage environment has expanded from the scientific laboratory through the business office to the home. In addition, functions performed have been extended from the serious statistical number crunching and manufacturing processes monitoring to video games and household kitchen recipes. What we are witnessing in the 1980s is a progressively deeper entrenchment of computer applications into the work life as well as domestic life of most Americans. According to Englebert Kirchner,[10] ten million office employees in the United States work with video terminals. It is conceivable that by the late 1980s, 50% of middle class Americans will own home computers.

A third observation concerns the decrease in the growth rates of the large computers. As will be discussed later, small computers, particularly the micro desk top computers, are growing at a faster rate than either the mainframes or minicomputers. Among the major factors which have contributed to this tendency are the financial stringency of the early 1980s, relative cheapness, ease of use and portability of the desk top computers. These factors will be elaborated later in the chapter.

A fourth observation concerns the brands of computer hardware. New brands of computers or old models with more sophisticated enhancements are virtually flooding the market. With the advent of cheaper, more user friendly and portable micros, this trend should continue through the 1980s. The profusion of new creations is demonstrated very clearly at the annual National Computer Conference (NCC). At the Houston

Texas NCC in June 1982 a delegate interviewed by *Computer World* reflected what will be a continuous dilemma of the 1980s when he said that "a person looking for a small business system or microcomputer might be confused by the number of offerings on the floor."[11]

Finally, there is the concept of user friendliness. Computer hardware and software marketers are constantly hyping user friendliness. Professional salesmen are renowned for having perfected the art of exaggeration. The author's hands-on experience with so-called user friendly software indicates that user friendliness sometimes depends on how much the user already knows about computer operations. Some of the application packages are assembled in a hurry to enable the vendor to have a market share of a rapidly expanding industry. For maximum utilization of these packages, basic knowledge of programming is usually assumed. In addition, there is the problem of the "fit" between the hardware-software package and a user's specific set of operations. In several cases, high expectations and confidence built into the user by advertising and oversell lead to frustration. This is particularly true when the computer hardware-software package makes an imperfect "fit" with user needs.

Hardware Growth Rates

In terms of dollars, mainframe computers continue to form the largest dollar segment of the computer industry. Recent spurts in the interest for small computers blurs this fact. In the early 1980s, U.S. worldwide shipments of the large scale mainframes hovered around the $18 billion mark. Due to the increasing sophistication of small computers, however, there has been a gradual downward off load of functions from large to small computers. This in effect means that a lot of data processing functions which used to be performed by mainframes are now done by minis or even micros. Consequently, the growth rate for mainframes is estimated to be around 5-8% through 1985. As Table 3 indicates, mainframes are likely to have the slowest growth rate for the industry in the 1980s.

International Business Machines (IBM) Corporation is still king in the installed base of worldwide mainframes. It commands more than 60 percent of the mainframe market and has for a considerable time acted as the standard setter for assessing other corporations' mainframe performance. Partly because of the rising popularity of smaller com-

Sector	Approximate Growth Rate %
Mainframe computers	5-8
Mini computers	30-35
Micro computers	50-60
Office Automation Systems	30-35
Data Communication Systems	30-35
Information Services	25-30

Table 3. Estimated Information Industry Growth Rates through 1985

puters, IBM's industrial supremacy is gradually being effectively challenged. Its share of the computer industry revenues has decreased in recent years. For instance, in 1979 it had 47 percent of the total sales of *Datamation's* 100. This percentage dropped to 40.6 percent and 38.8 percent in 1980 and 1981 respectively.[12]

As regards minicomputers, worldwide shipments in the early 1980s have been estimated at around $6 to $8 billion. As discussed in Chapter 2, there has been a gradual "growing up" into the mainframe turf by minicomputers. This came about by the introduction and marketing of the so-called "super minis" in the 1970s. Such machines have had increased computer capacities to the extent of replacing mainframes in some corporations. The main suppliers of super minis were originally Digital Equipment Corporation, Perkin-Elmer, and Prime Computer. The ranks have been expanded to include Data General, Hewlett-Packard, Honeywell, and a host of other corporations.

In spite of the super minis, some analysts have argued that the minicomputer sector is bound to grow slower than it was anticipated in the 1970s. John Verity[13] stipulated that many of the applications which have been traditionally performed by minicomputers can be done as efficiently and more cost-effectively by microcomputers. Among the functions cited are: manufacturing process control, data collection, interactive video, and stand alone business processing. This trend is becoming more apparent with the increasing sophistication of micro computers. One of the disadvantages of micros when they were introduced in the 1970s was lack of software. Since then, independent software companies (independent of hardware manufacturers) have developed several application packages for micros. Using these packages, users will most certainly drift away from minis to micros.

Digital Equipment Corporation (DEC) still leads in this industrial sector with regard to the installed base. As for the rest of corporations' share of the mini market the first ten rankings other than DEC have been fluctuating in the last five years. Like the mainframe sector, this indicates the volatile nature of the computer industry. Corporations in the current first ten rankings may not be in that top ten by 1985.

Microcomputers are having a tremendous impact on the data processing scene. Professional literature variously refers to them as desktop, personal, or simply microcomputers. They are characterized by portability, relative ease of operation, low cost, and increasing availability of multipurpose applications packages. They are thus ideal for small scale businesses—classrooms, small scale information centers or libraries, and homes. The microcomputer industrial sector is estimated to have a growth rate of 50-60% through 1985. Their total revenue of $1.9 billion in 1980 is relatively small compared with minis or mainframes.

While Apple Computer Corporation has been the sector leader for some time, the follow up companies are not as far behind the first place as is the case for mainframes with IBM leadership or minis with Digital Equipment Corporation. With the recent introduction of IBM's personal computer and Digital Equipment's desk top series into the sector, competition for the desk top market is becoming more fierce.

As Figure 9 indicates, the proliferation of micro computers will make computer services accessible to almost every able bodied American by 1985. With special communications packages, micro computers are transformed into remote terminals which can connect with distant computer centers. In other words, desk top computers can not only perform small scale personalized operations, but they can be used to access institutional data banks at remote locations. Such versatility and convenience of use partly explain the popularity of microcomputers.

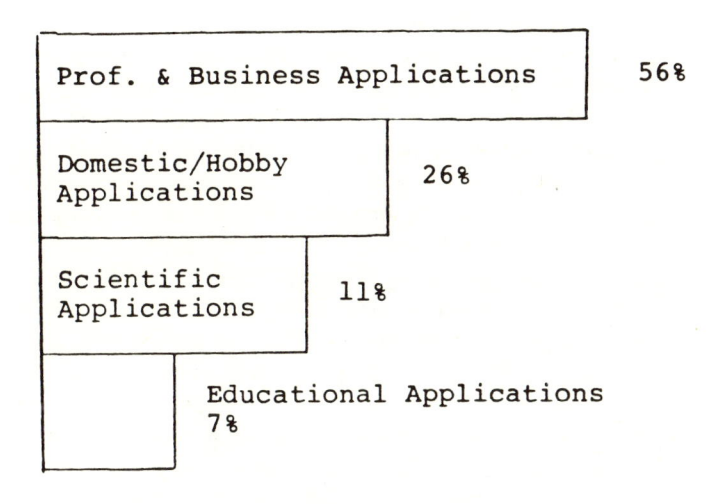

```
┌─────────────────────────────────────┐
│ Prof. & Business Applications       │   56%
├──────────────────────────┬──────────┘
│ Domestic/Hobby           │
│ Applications             │   26%
├───────────────────┬──────┘
│ Scientific        │
│ Applications      │   11%
├───────┬───────────┘
│       │  Educational Applications
│       │  7%
└───────┘
```

Figure 9. Estimated Microcomputer Installation through 1985

The Software Sector

As partly discussed in Chapter 2, software are programs which instruct computers how to perform specific operations. Initially, such programs were sold by computer manufacturers as accessories to a complete computer system. Such arrangements were referred to as "bundled" packages. Selling hardware and software as separate packages, or "unbundling," became necessary for a number of reasons. First, miniaturization of hardware components made hardware cheaper than before. Automation of production processes and eventual mass production of components further reduced costs of hardware. Second, the broadening of the computer user base resulted in demand for sophisticated applications requiring complicated programs. Since programming is labor intensive, software ended up being more expensive than hardware. Finally, due to increased demand for computer services, it became speedier to have software developed by specialist software houses. As a result, most computer manufacturers sold software and hardware as separate items.

Analysts of the software-hardware relationship often use the phrase "the tail wags the dog" to indicate the change in relative importance of software versus hardware. Some have asserted that by the late 1980s software may be so expensive compared to hardware that computer manufacturers might reach a stage whereby computer systems are priced in such a way as to sell software and give away hardware free!

Software dollar volume is difficult to separate from total revenues as it is usually lumped together with hardware. In the early 1980s, IBM was the leader in software revenues which were estimated at $4.5 billion.[14] Digital Equipment, Sperry Corporation, and Computer Sciences Corporation each had software revenues in excess of $.5 billion. The software growth rate is estimated at around 27 percent annually through 1985. At that rate, it should constitute approximately 25 percent of the computer industry by 1985.

Of special significance to the software sector has been the development of microcomputers. Due to the diversity of applications required of micros, several independent software houses have sprouted on the scene to take advantage of the market. Generalized packages like VisiCalc, CalcStar, WordStar, and DataStar have been marketed. With slight modifications such packages may be used on a variety of microcomputers. It is estimated that by 1985, the market for microcomputer software will be approximately $2 billion.

Thus software "unbundling" has resulted in the tendency for users to have a motley of packages to choose from. It is no longer mandatory for a user to accept the hardware vendor's software. In addition, largely due to competition, the price of application packages has been remarkably reduced.

Information Services

The information revolution has spawned several small industries.[15] What Wall Street usually refers to as computer services is a wide sweep which includes software. The information services sector has been growing rapidly and was around $15 billion in the early 1980s. Industry forecasters estimate that it will expand at a rate of about 10 percent per year to reach $35 billion in 1985.

Our approach excludes software but embraces essentially significant spin-offs or by-products of the mainstream of the computer industry. For analytical purposes, two broad categories will be identified. In the first place, there are data processing services. Such services would include programming, data entry and processing for institutions without computer facilities or for larger organizations whose data processing departments are inadequate. Secondly, there is the category of databases, whereby on-line databases are made accessible to institutions or individuals.

Whereas these two categories are not necessarily mutually exclusive, data processing services firms tend to employ more programmers and data entry personnel. In addition, such firms do in effect accomplish what an inhouse data processing department would have done given an ideal situation. In other words, one of their prime functions is to serve as buffers to carry the excess load of large scale data processing departments in the U.S. Federal Government, state governments and private institutions.

Two types of user needs are satisfied by data processing services. One category of users whose needs are catered to are the large government departments (federal, state or city) or large corporations whose data processing departments cannot accommodate all internal data processing requirements. For this category of users, data processing corporations provide fast and effective processing of jobs with critical deadlines. A second type of user need emanates from small and medium sized firms with no computer facilities. By farming out their data processing requirements to specialist computer services corporations, they are able to computerize some of their functions with no investment in hardware, software and computer personnel.

Data processing services are rendered by several types of corporations. Two loosely separated categories can be discerned. First, there are independent firms which specialize in these services. Among these leading companies include Computer Sciences Corporation and Automatic Data Processing. Second, there are divisions or branches of large corporations with excess computing expertise and capacity. Among the latter are: Citibank, Mellon Bank, Boeing, McDonnell Douglas and General Electric. The independents tend to cater to a diversity of industries whereas corporation divisions tend to be industry specific. For instance Mellon Bank and Citibank cater to financial institutions whereas Automatic Data Processing has a diversified clientele.

On-line Database Services

As part of the information technological development discussed in Chapter 2, it is now possible to use computers to store and retrieve masses of information. Databases are some of the byproducts of the information revolution. On-line databases are banks of information that have been processed, stored, and made retrievable by electronic devices. As will be discussed in Chapter 5, the development of huge databases may be both a bane and a blessing for the information user. They do not necessarily provide new information. Some of the information they contain may be concurrently available in a "hard copy" format or the printed form. A number of indexes are available in both forms. For instance: *Engineering Index Monthly* is available on-line as Compendex; the *Education Index* (hard copy) is available as part of the ERIC database; *Excerpta Medica*, an index for medical sciences is now available on EMBASE database. Similarly, LEXIS database contains court decisions which are available in published legal documents. In recent years, database development has expanded to cover a very wide range of subjects.

Because of this trend of development, "everything you always wanted to know may soon be on-line."[16] This will undoubtedly be an advantage *if* you can afford the fee levied by the database vendor! The question of whether one can afford the charges may not only be relevant to individuals with no institutional support. Some of the small firms may also find it too expensive to procure relevant material from some high priced data banks. On the other hand, for business executives or high-ranking government officials, or professionals like lawyers and pharmacists, data banks are becoming invaluable. Such professionals cannot afford to operate without them.

Whatever the case for an information user, the rationale for resorting to the data bank as an information source revolves around the question of human problem solving. For corporations, government, or even individuals, decision-making is a delicate process of balancing given facts, prior expectations, and future outcomes. We are constantly faced with decision making situations when we need a lot of accurate information. According to Garvin, "When there is a problem, 90 percent of the work is in finding the source and 10 percent of the work is in using the source material to get the answer."[17] While we may not agree with the percentages, his comment underscores the importance of speedy access to information in problem solving. Ideally, databases are meant to reduce the time taken in locating relevant information for decision making.

Using a computer terminal as an access point, a lawyer can get an immediate printout of the full text of a federal or state court decision stored on Mead Corporation's LEXIS data bank on law literature. Likewise, a business executive can get price quotations on stocks, bonds, options and mutual funds from Dow Jones News Retrieval Online Service. As for a graduate research student in need of literature search, a number of bibliographic services have been developed which serve as on-line literature guides. DIALOG and ORBIT bibliographic services supplied by Lockheed Corporation and Systems Development Corporation respectively, are some of the common ones. Table 4 gives a select sample of on-line database services. For a comprehensive listing of databases, Martha Williams' *Computer-Readable Databases: A Directory and Data Sourcebook*[18] is an outstanding source, which includes international corporations. Williams indicated that the number of available databases increased from 528 in 1979 to 773 in 1982, showing a 55 percent increase. As for industrial forecasts, total revenues generated by databases are expected to reach $2.99 billion in 1985.[19] This dollar volume will be reached at an annual growth rate of approximately 30 percent.

There are currently over 270 producers and vendors of databases. Two categories of database producers may be identified. There is first the not-for-profit organizations, composed of professional societies, federal agencies, and research institutions. Among the most prominent producers are the American Chemical Society, the National Technical Information Service (NTIS of the U.S. Department of Commerce), the American Institute of Physics, the American Society of Metals, Engineering Information Inc. (formerly Engineering Index Inc.), the Institute of Textile Technology, the American Psychological Association, the National Library of Medicine, and the American Geological Institute. Some universities also produce databases.

Second, there is the commercial source of databases. As is typical of new computer based services, several companies large and small are vying for a market share of the database market. The current trend is the increasing interest and participation of multinational giant corporations. Many of the giants are entering the market through acquisition of smaller database producing companies. For instance in 1979, McGraw-Hill Corporation acquired Data Resources Inc. and in 1981, Burroughs Corporation acquired Systems Development Corporation.[20]

As regards mode of operation, some of the commercial organizations buy databases from not-for-profit organizations and modify them for their own purposes. At the same time, they generate their own databases. Among the leading firms are: Lockheed Aircraft Corporation, Predicasts

Data Base	Producer	Contents	Suppliers	Price
Lexis	Mead Corporation	Full text of federal and state court decisions, statutes etc.	Mead Corporation	$500 monthly for one terminal + $60-90 per hour
Dow Jones News Retrieval Service	Dow Jones	Articles from the Wall Street Journal, Barrons and Dow Jones News Service + price quotations for stocks, bonds, mutual funds and options.	Dow Jones Co. GTE Bunker Ramo Corp. Telerante Systems Inc.	$50 per user $40 per hour
Promt	Predicasts Inc.	Abstracts, citations on technology, markets and new products.	Lockheed Corp. Systems Development Corp.	$90 per connect hour
Medline	National Library of Medicine	Biomedical literature: citations, abstracts of U.S. and international journals.	BRS Lockheed	$16 per hour $35 per hour
NTIS	National Technical Information Service (U.S. Dept. of Commerce)	Citations, abstracts of unclassified reports of federal research projects.	Systems Development Corp. Lockheed BRS	$27-44 per hour from BRS, $35 from Lockheed and SDC
New York Times Information Bank	New York Times Co.	Abstracts of New York Times and selected newspapers and magazines.	New York Times Co.	$80-100 per hour
Japanese Economic Information Service	Data Resources Inc.	Data on the Japanese economy and forecasts	Data Resources Inc.	$6,400 annual subscription + computer time

Table 4. Selected Database Samples

Inc., Chase Manhattan, Citicorp, Mead Corporation, Xerox, the New York Times Company, Dow Jones, Burroughs Corporation, Boeing and Nexus Corporation. The industry is very dynamic and new firms are created almost every year. What is interesting about the participating companies is the range of their industrial base. Publishers, banks, computer manufacturers, and aircraft industry giants are heavily represented. Their main link appears to be that their industrial bases are information intensive. In other words, to function effectively as business corporations, they need a tremendous amount of fast up-to-date information.

Subject coverage is extremely varied within databases. The earliest databases were developed by government agencies,[21] such as the National Aeronautical and Space Administration (NASA) and the Atomic Energy Commission (AEC), now the Energy Research and Development Administration (ERDA). Initially, the hard sciences like physics, electronics, and electrical engineering were covered. Interest spread to the so-called "soft sciences" namely psychology, education, and other social sciences. Within the last few years, coverage has been extended to economics, finance, law and a host of other subjects.

THE INFORMATION MARKET AND MARKET SEGMENTATION

For the purposes of this text, the definition of the term "market" as it appears in the *Marketing Handbook* will be adopted thus: "Within marketing, the market is the potential demand for a physical good or service—that is, markets are people with purchasing power."[22] Considered in a wider context, the majority of the U.S. population may be deemed to constitute the information market. Within the purview of the present work, however, the market is composed of those individuals or institutions which are actual or potential users of information centers and libraries or purchase information processing equipment, especially computers. It is thus very heterogeneous and difficult to divide into small segments. Business analysts[23, 24] advocate market segmentation to facilitate rational market strategy while developing products for customers. In addition, some information scientists and librarians like Dragon,[25] Elias[26] and Weinstock[27] have strongly supported the application of the market segmentation principle to information.

We are in the information business. Other than hardware, several of the information products and services tend to be intangible. The intangibility of products should not bar information analysts from using appropriate terms which are standard parlance in business. With this in mind we shall give an overview of the U.S. information market. Typically two subcategories may be identified, the industrial market and the consumer market. Each of the subcategories has various market segments. Detailed information needs of segments and access to information will be discussed in Chapter 5.

The Industrial Market

In this category, information is consumed as a resource used in manufacturing other commercial goods. When Westinghouse Electric Corporation, Exxon Corporation or Johnson and Johnson use PROMT data base produced by Predicasts Inc. and get information on competitors' new products, technology, or markets, they incur indirect costs. Such costs are part of the industrial process and absorbed in the prices they charge their customers.

Segmentation of this sector may be by size of the corporation or the nature of the basic industry of the organization. In its segmentation procedure an information center (say Dow Jones) may have as client segments banking and finance, pharmaceuticals, automobile and aircraft industries. The information needs, analysis and packaging would be different for each of these industries.

The industrial market has a number of characteristics which are significant to the information industry. First, it has a very high demand for information products; it is common for a corporation to pay up to $50,000 for a market survey package. Second, it has a strong and steady purchasing power. This tends to inflate prices for computerized on-line services. Finally, it has expertise in selection and evaluation of information products. Through its patronage, this category has supported some information industries like databases. But at the same time, data vendors have hiked prices beyond the reach of small firms or individuals who might need to utilize the same services.

The Consumer Market

This is composed of information products consumers who are "end users" and do not use it to produce other products. It is a very broad category with multifarious interests. Segmentation can be attempted based on income, educational attainment or professional affiliation.

Surveys conducted in the U.S. indicate that the predominant user of the American public library is from the middle class. Another consistent user is the high school and college student. Current computer based information services require a degree of sophistication which is also middle class oriented. Finally, the trend toward home computers which will pervade the domestic environments will extend use to the blue collar home, especially with the video game mania of the 1980s.

In the 1980s, the information consumer market is likely to remain predominantly middle class. While its purchase power may not be as high as the industrial market's, it will have substantial discretionary income to spend on information products and services.

Information Market Operators

The 1980s are witnessing the development of several business enterprises, some of which are very small, to siphon the lucrative information market. The mainstream of the information market whereby hardware is marketed is like any other business. Information services have expanded to beget a variety of new operators with new titles.

The term wholesale could be applied to the producer or vendor of databases who does not sell directly to the end user. The middlemen, who in other businesses are simply retailers, have coined for themselves terms like information brokers or counselors. Due to the increasing complexity of information sources, these middlemen have developed expertise on how to locate, analyze and package information for the end user. They conduct literature searches on almost any subject and furnish the requested information in a very short time. Information counselor or brokerage firms purchase their information from data banks. Such firms are common in large U.S. cities like New York, Chicago, Washington, D.C. and Los Angeles. As alternative sources of information, they are the greatest challenge to the library in its traditional form.

The Information Industry Association

Formed in 1968 in Washington, D.C., the Information Industry Association is one of the indices of the growing importance of information services in the business world. A *Publishers Weekly* report said that, "it was formed to represent business firms which create, supply and distribute information services, particularly those using the more advanced forms of information technology."[28] Its objectives are: (a) To make customers aware of members' services. (b) To cause "a change in the way people react to the industry." (c) To promote the industry in a manner that will avoid "oversell."[29] Its services are comparable to the standard trade association.

IMPLICATIONS FOR INFORMATION CENTERS AND LIBRARIES

Several implications may be discerned from this chapter. In the first place, due to the miniaturization of computer hardware and the concomitant reduction in prices, more people will be using computers as daily information source tools through the 1980s. Second, other than increased computer expertise there will be an increase in the number of access points. Third, the demand for on-line services will go up. Fourth, the increase in the number of independent database searches for a fee (counselors or brokers) will pose an impregnable challenge to information centers and libraries as sources of information.

At its present rate of development, the information industry will soon furnish the information professional hundreds of options to choose from. One of the commonest brain teasers for managers of information centers will be which one do we buy? For services, it may not matter whereas for hardware or software it would help to know whether the vendor will be in business a few years from now to modify or repair the product if necessary. Finally, with all the wonders of computer technology at our disposal are we serving the user needs or are we simply satisfying our ego as masters of modern technology? Chapter 5 will attempt to address these issues.

NOTES

1. Marc Uri Porat, *The Information Economy* (Washington, D.C.: Government Printing Office, 1977).

2. Fei Xiaotong, "Glimpses of America," *Datamation* 26 (May 1980):234-40.

3. Bernard Ostry, "The Information Revolution. Hard Choices for Canada's Future," *Canadian Library Journal* (April 1980), p. 88.

4. Alan L. Frohman, "Technology as a Competitive Weapon," *Harvard Business Review* 60 (January-February 1982):97.

5. John F. Rockart and Michael E. Treacy, "The CEO Goes On-line," *Harvard Business Review* 60 (January-February 1982):82-88.

6. *Standard and Poor's Industry Surveys N-Z* (April 1982), p. O21.

7. Leopold Froehlich, "Robots to the Rescue?," *Datamation* 27 (January 1981):86.

8. *Ibid.*, p. 85.

9. Alan Gilpin, *Dictionary of Economic Terms* (London: Butterworths, 1973), p. 107.

10. Englebert Kirchner, "At the Mercy of Machines," *Datamation* 28 (September 1982):252-61.

11. Tim Scannel, "Under NCC Big Top, Professionalism Grows," *Computer World* 16 (June 14, 1982):1.

12. Pamela Archbold, "The Foremost U.S. Companies in the Data Processing Industry," *Datamation* 28 (June 1982):122.

13. John W. Verity, "Alas, Poor Mini," *Datamation* 28 (September 1982):224,228.

14. Pamela Archbold, "The Foremost...":120.

15. Alfred R. Berkeley, "Millionaire Machine," *Datamation* 27 (August 1981):21-22.

16. Walter Kiechel III, "Everything You Always Wanted to Know May Soon Be On-line," *Fortune* 101 (May 5, 1980):226-40.

17. A. P. Garvin, *How to Win With Information or Lose Without It* (Washington, D.C.: Bermont Books, 1980), p. 45.

18. Martha Williams, *Computer Readable Databases: A Directory and Data Sourcebook* (Washington, D.C.: American Society for Information Science, 1982), p. viii.

19. Deborah Sojka, "Database Booming," *Datamation* 27 (March 1981):96.

20. Peter Wright, "The Datamation 100: The Top 100 U.S. Companies in the DP Industry," *Datamation* 27 (June 1981):91.

21. Martha Williams, "Databases—A History of Development and Trends from 1966 through 1975," *Journal of the American Society for Information Science* 28 (1977):71-78.

22. Albert Wesley Frey, *Marketing Handbook* 2d ed. (New York: Ronald Press Company, 1965), p. 13.

23. Edward Cundiff, et. al., *Fundamentals of Modern Marketing* (Englewood Cliffs, N.J.: Prentice-Hall, 1976), pp. 9-19.
Cycle.

24. Philip Kotler, *Marketing for Nonprofit Organizations* (Englewood Cliffs, N.J.: Prentice-Hall, 1975), pp. 56-61.

25. Andrea Dragon, "Marketing the Library," *Wilson Library Bulletin* 53 (March 1979):498-500.

26. Art Elias, "Marketing for Online Bibliographical Services," *Scientific and Technical Information Online Reviews* 3 (March 1979):110-14.

27. M. Weinstock, "Marketing Library and Information Service," in *Encyclopedia of Library and Information Science*, vol. 17 (New York: Marcel Dekker, 1976): 165-188.

28. "Information Industry Association Formed," *Publishers Weekly* 194 (November 18, 1968):60.

29. "The Information Market," *Publishers Weekly* 195 (April 14, 1969):67.

5
User Access to Information

Users of management information centers, data banks, libraries or any other type of information center seek information to satisfy specific needs. Industrialized countries have developed sophisticated systems to process and store information in order to satisfy those needs. We may refer to such sources as societal information systems. Within the U.S. context, several examples abound. Currently, information from such sources is issued mainly in "hard copy" printed form or via computer-based on-line retrieval systems. Among the most commonly used examples of the "hard copy" type are the Federal Register and AT&T's Yellow Pages. The former makes available to the public federal regulations and legal notices issued by the Executive Branch of the U.S. Federal Government, while the latter contains a list of business enterprises in an area listed by product. As for on-line systems, MEDLINE containing medical literature, Lockheed DIALOG which is a general bibliographic index and LEXIS containing Federal and state court decisions are some of the common ones.

At the corporation level, data processing departments or divisions have over the years developed computer-based information centers for internal use. As presently constituted, these centers contain information which reflects the operations of a given corporation. Some industrial giants like IBM, Johnson and Johnson and Citicorp have large masses of information in these systems. Similar systems have been established for public institutions like state, city and large county administrations. Within the institutional confines, information systems ordinarily serve the information needs of the employees of a given institution.

84   The Information Dilemma

User access as explored in this chapter is the interface between user needs and societal or institutional information systems. Information professionals match user needs with information in societal or institutional information systems. In other words, they are facilitators of user access to information. As discussed in previous chapters, the past two decades have witnessed increasing computerization of information systems. The 1980s are witnessing further advances in information technology and yet more computerization of information processes. Inevitably, problems have developed vis-à-vis user access.

While highlighting the dilemma of charging fees for information, the main thrust of this chapter centers around the following topics:

1. Information and Decision Making
2. Information Monopoly and Power
3. Information Seeking Behavior
4. Identification of User Needs for Information
5. Scope of User Access to Information
6. Dilemma of User Access to Information
7. Attempts to Solve User Access Problems

INFORMATION AND DECISION MAKING

The magnitude of the importance of user access to the right information, at the right time, in the right place and in the right format is underscored by the fundamental tenet of human existence—making a decision. We are constantly faced with making decisions every day of our lives. For every single decision we make, more than one piece of information is needed in order to examine a number of possible alternatives and arrive at a final decision. Essentially decision making is analogous to problem solving. For instance a homemaker (housewife) with a problem deciding whether to buy a generic or branded product might resort to a neighbor's advice, *Consumer Reports* magazine, or any other source of information. Likewise, professionals, government officials, research students, and/or business executives grapple with their problems by resorting to institutional or societal information systems.

Decision theory analysts have advanced several models of decision making. One of the most relevant theories in day-to-day decision making appears to be the "satisficing decision model." As Harold Leavitt[1] explained we usually indulge in a limited search for relevant information; we formulate alternatives and select the satisfactory rather than the optimal. Most decision makers make decisions under constraints and even if the hypothetical optimal decision were identifiable, the satisfactory decision may be selected. This is implicit in most decisions we make. As Figure 10 indicates, whatever decision model we select, the information input is vital and goes through three basic stages INPUT → PROCESS → OUTPUT. The information input is vital for the final decision and access to appropriate information is invaluable.

One of the most perplexing phenomena of modern society has been referred to as "runaway technology." Most people in industrialized countries find themselves working in environments where technology is rapidly changing. This phenomenon further accentuates the need to have access to the right information promptly with a minimum "hassle." Slater and Bennis clearly characterized this phenomenon when they said, "We are now beginning an era when a man's knowledge and approach can become obsolete before he has even begun the career for which he was trained. The value of what one learns is slipping away, like the value of money in runaway inflation. We are living in an era which could be characterized as a runaway inflation of knowledge and skill."[2] This phenomenon puts on-line databases at a very high premium for professionals and skilled technicians. In order to make rational decisions, professionals, business executives and public administrators must keep abreast of current developments. Due to runaway technology one has, as it were, to run very hard to keep in one spot. As discussed in Chapter 4, it is now possible to retrieve up-to-the-minute information from some on-line data banks. Consequently, the mode of access, the price of access and the ease of access become vital issues for the information user.

INFORMATION MONOPOLY AND POWER

While the maxim "information is power" might be overstretched, it has been plausibly argued that possession of vital information at the right moment may lead to acquisition or enhancement of power. In this context, power is defined as the ability to influence other people's actions. Some critics have pointed out that lack of relevant information is particularly harmful in the decision making process.[3] During the Information Age, individual survival, sustenance and success will de-

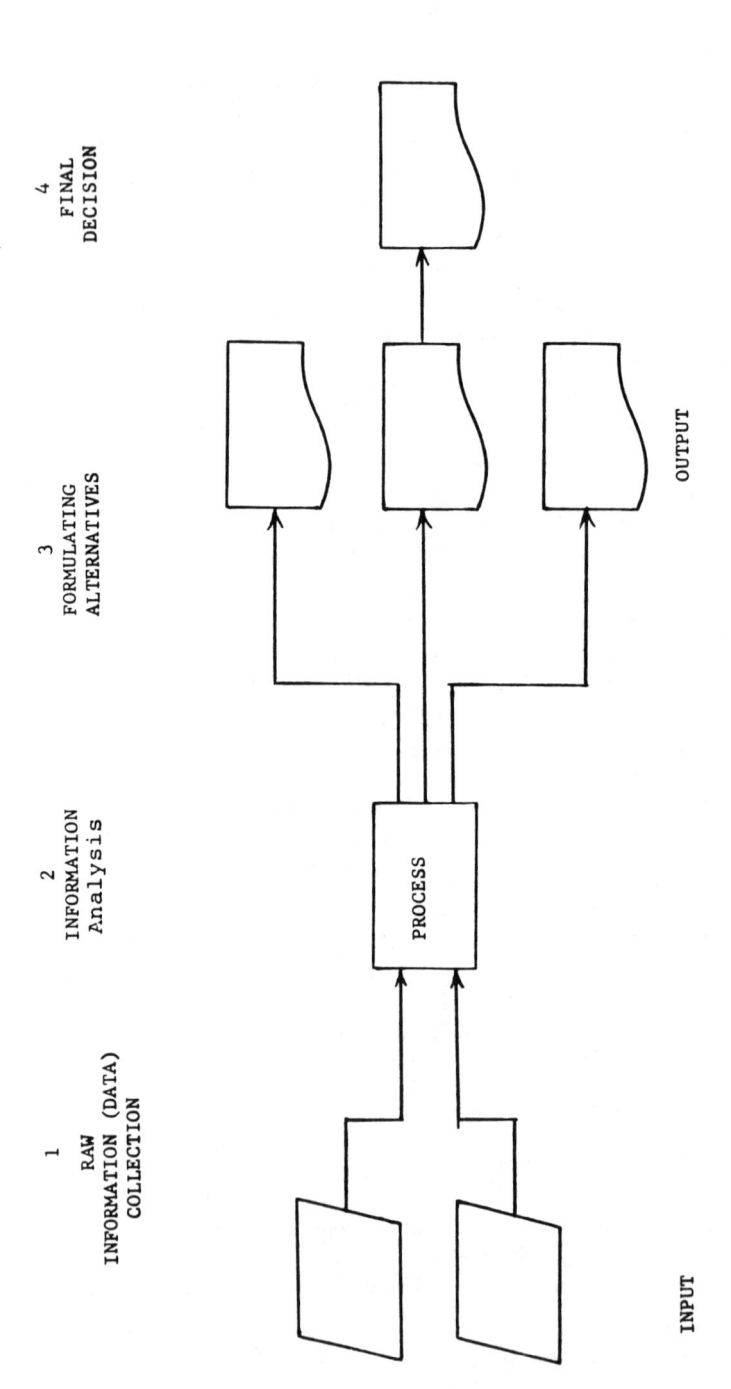

Figure 10. Decision Model with Information Input

pend on the quality and quantity of information one can acquire. As a corollary to information acquisition, the magnitude of power it confers may also depend on the expertise with which it is applied or wielded. As Garvin intimated, "The future in fact, promises to bring an environment in which the people who know how to acquire, store, access, distribute and control information stand to have more power than they have ever had before in the history of mankind."[4]

Information as a source of power is more manifest in executive suites of large business corporations than other institutions. Business leaders are finding it more difficult to survive due to the increased internationalization of trade and commerce. Local markets which were once sacred turfs have been invaded by Japanese and other aggressive multinational corporations. Whether we consider large or small corporations, however, success and power will be predicated on how accurate and current is an institution's information on:

1. *Markets*
- Local or international
- Size in terms of approximate numbers of people with effective purchasing power
- Demographic distribution
- Segmentation as it affects product differentiation and development

2. *Competitors*
- Local or international
- Marketing strategies and probable areas of comparable advantage
- Product deployment and lines
- Management style
- Financial resources and effectiveness

3. *Relevant Technology*
- As applicable to local or international markets
- How to acquire appropriate techniques
- Research and development needed

4. *Government Regulations*
- Local or international
- Effects on product development
- Effects on marketing strategies
- Lobbying techniques to evade or postpone vital pending regulations

Business analysts[5] have aptly warned about the advent of information imperialism. Such imperialism prevails when large corporations which have ample access to computerized data banks have a definite competitive edge over smaller commercial enterprises. In practical terms, it boils down to whether a firm can afford a $100,000 Data Resources Inc. econometrics sales forecast package for a product, say computer chips, in the midwest U.S. or Venezuela. Alternatively, a corporation may opt to subscribe to Predicasts Inc. on-line database, Promt, which gives current information on markets and new products at $90 per connect hour.

Politically and socially, power may be wielded by possession of unique information. Such power is evident especially at election time. Well researched public opinion polls would indicate to prospective candidates whether and in what constituency to run for election. In the United States context, presidential, gubernatorial, and local elections are expensive to undertake. The ultimate cost and frustration which emanate from the election campaign can be minimized by prior possession of relevant information about constituents and their demographic characteristics. While the possession of extraneous information may be wielded by individuals, institutional information monopoly is more pervasive, effective and powerful. This is largely due to the information networking effect. For instance, the U.S. Democratic and Republican parties are more effective than the individual candidates in acquiring and utilizing the information power. By using local, regional, and national bases, they set up coordinated computer-based networks to monitor the trend of the campaigns.

Information monopoly will reach critical proportions during the Information Age. In the 1980s the dilemma will come when most of the fundamental information relevant for survival is packaged and sold at a high price. As an example, if one wants his or her child to acquire elementary reading or math skills, teach-yourself packages will be available on cartridges or floppy disks. Inevitably one has to acquire a microcomputer or some other electronic device in order to use the package. It is also conceivable that a lot of the information now available in encyclopedias will be available on-line or in machine readable packages, and thus less accessible to people who cannot afford the price.

It was partly because of the threat of this monopoly that the White House Conference on Library and Information Services was convened in Washington, D.C. in 1979. The conference was indeed a microcosm of the U.S. society. Computer and communications industries giants like IBM, Warner Communications, Tymshare and Texas Instruments were well represented. Information professionals working in information centers and libraries formed the majority of delegates. According to the conference report, "Delegates made it clear that they believed access to information is power, and that in our democratic society the people themselves want to decide how to use that power."[6]

As an *ad hoc* societal entity, the conference was the nearest to the whole U.S. body politic's reaction to the problems of the Information Age. All the user access issues raised in this chapter were discussed. As indicated in the final report one of the composite questions delegates attempted to address was, "When should information be private, when should it be without cost and how should freedom of information principles be applied?"[7]

INFORMATION SEEKING BEHAVIOR

The rationale or motivation for seeking information usually predicates the individual's information seeking behavior. Why access an information source? How to access an information source? Is the information sought worth the price? Responses to these questions are relevant in assessing a person's information seeking behavior and ultimately the willingness to pay a fee for information.

For individuals, there are no standard responses to these questions. That is human nature, full of personal idiosyncracies, goals and objectives in life and shaped by social upbringing. However, it is persuasive to have recourse to Abraham Maslow's theory on personality and motivation[8] for part of the answers. From an ordinary person's point of view, motivation to access an information source may be deemed to satisfy a hierarchy of needs promulgated by Maslow as indicated in Figure 11.

At the bottom of the pyramid are basic needs like having food, shelter and daily requirements for survival. Needs get sophisticated as one moves up the pyramid. During the Information Age, the centrifugal forces of information as a pivot for personal achievement will make it invaluable at each level of the hierarchy. As an illustration, today in industrialized countries like Germany, Britain and the United States, one needs specialist information (skills) to survive beyond the poverty level. On the other hand, a member of the Rockefeller or Kennedy family (U.S.) or the Earl of Home (U.K.) does not need information for mere survival. He might need information to maintain his societal esteem or for aesthetics. In pursuit of the satisfaction of these needs,

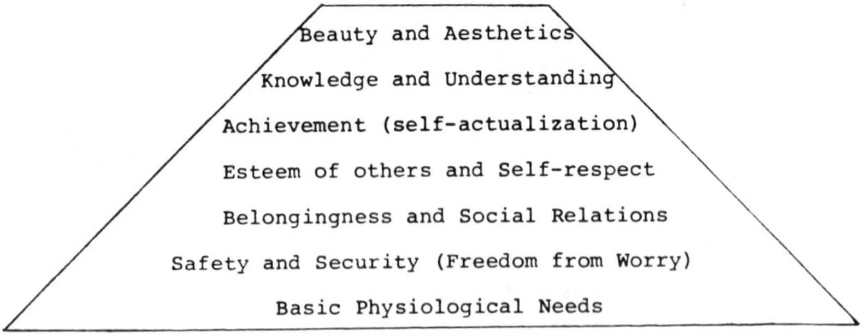

90 The Information Dilemma

```
        _____
       /Beauty and Aesthetics\
      /  Knowledge and Understanding\
     /  Achievement (self-actualization)\
    /    Esteem of others and Self-respect \
   /      Belongingness and Social Relations \
  /      Safety and Security (Freedom from Worry) \
 /              Basic Physiological Needs           \
/_____\
```

Figure 11. Maslow's Hierarchy of Human Needs

individuals will indulge in various types of information-seeking behaviors. Such behaviors might range from seeking information from acquaintances or free public information sources to business sources charging a fee.

This trend of thought correlates with Newell and Simon's theory which "...proclaims man to be an information processing system, at least when he is solving problems."[9] Within himself, man collects, sieves, or otherwise processes information in reaction to his environment. In their book entitled *Human Information Processing*, Lindsay and Norman[10] likewise underscore the importance of information in problem analysis and decision making. While accepting such analyses, we contend that information is not processed for its own sake. Our assertion in this text is that user access to information, which leads to human information processing, is related to personality and motivation.

Other scholars have subscribed to this theory linking user needs to information seeking behaviors. While T.D. Wilson's[11] approach is somewhat different, he recognizes the link between information needs and information-seeking behavior. As we resort to Maslow's or other psychologists' theories on motivation, however, we must be cognizant of the fact that they are theoretical constructs. We may thus not be able to use them with absolute precision to ascertain the cause-effect relationships between user and the information sought. It will suffice to regard them as probable guides.

INFORMATION AND USER NEEDS—
A PRAGMATIC APPROACH

It has already been implicitly posited that the individual's information requirements are a function of his basic needs for survival and self enrichment. However, individuals are members of variegated groups and subgroups which may be categorized as social, political, or economic and so forth. While the information needs of the individual may differ from a multi-national corporation, say Gulf Oil, IBM and Westinghouse, the fundamental purposes for gathering information are essentially the same. It may be argued that stripped to the bare minimum, the basic core centers around the need for self actualization in case of the individual, with the ultimate aim of optimizing one's potential. Similarly, the group aims at perfecting its strategic relationships and maximizing its impact vis-à-vis individuals or other groups. Artandi[12] supports this trend of argument and makes a slight distinction between group and individual information needs.

At the group level, James Oates[13] identified two basic needs regardless of the type of organization. First, an organization needs information about itself and its own operations. Second, it needs external information about its environment. Pearson stressed the needs and variability of information thus,

> ...it is "needs" which are the major determinant of the use and hence the value of information...these needs are influenced by the individual researcher, by the group of which he forms a part, and by the nature of the organization in which he is employed. These three factors affect the value of information, and as they can each have characteristics which may differ with time, it can be argued that information has a value which will vary with time at which it is received.[14]

In other words, "information need" is a dynamic feature of the information-transfer process. User access thus becomes a pragmatic attempt to satisfy that need.

THE SCOPE OF USER ACCESS TO INFORMATION

User access to information may be analyzed at two levels. First, there is the micro level, whereby it is examined in respect to information systems design. The basic question to ask at this level is "Does the system as designed contain intrinsic obstacles to user access?" Second, there is the macro level which concerns access to societal information systems. Pertinent questions at the macro level are centered around legal, economic, and social barriers to user access.

While user access is one of the most vital concepts in information systems design, system designers are usually so engrossed in technical detail that they often overlook this fact. Generally, at the micro level, information systems are designed for an institution or people in a given locale. Some of the fundamental questions we should pose are:

1. For whom are we designing the system?
2. How appropriate is the access medium or language?
3. Have we considered ergonomics—i.e., human physical factors?
4. Is the system flexible enough to accommodate future modifications?

In several cases, micro information systems are designed for the convenience of the operator and not the ultimate user. As we move deeply into the information driven society, competition for clients is gradually forcing designers to consider user oriented systems. As discussed in Chapter 3, so called "user friendly" systems are being designed with user ease of use in mind.

Two simple illustrations will show irritations that may serve as barriers to manual or computer-based systems. In a traditional library with a card catalog, one usually finds guides on how to use the library. The one page guide on how to use the card catalog may start by telling you that the library is now using the AACR II Rules and the whole system has been recatalogued. The user might retort "Who cares about AACR II? All I need is Jimmy Carter's autobiography."

As for a computer-based system in an insurance corporation, say Prudential Insurance Corporation, an insurance executive may need to retrieve a client's records from the internal corporation's data bank. After the preliminaries of getting on the system, the executive may get a message: "You are now connected to the PRUDO relational database..." She may likewise retort "So what! I don't care whether the database is relational, all I need are Sarah Meyer's records!"

In both cases the information system designer wanted the "world" to know that the system is using up to date methods. Presumably this is the "professional" world of data processors or librarians. On the other hand, the overworked insurance executive or congressman seeking information has her or his own profession to attend to!

At the macro level, user access to societal information systems is progressively being affected by increasing computerization. This text has stressed the gradual "locking up" of vital information in computer-based data banks. As we get even more sophisticated, will the bona fide researcher with scanty funds or a college student with minimal discretionary income have access to these information banks?

As we consider whether or how to price our information products and services, we should simultaneously consider whether our systems maximize user access to information. Our esteem and integrity as information professionals will ultimately depend on how effectively do we facilitate such access to the relevant information.

THE FEES CONTROVERSY

Our discussions so far have centered around the rapid growth of the information market and industry with emphasis on the United States scene. Many of the concepts analyzed are, however, relevant to other industrialized countries especially Western Europe. The increased use of the computer in information handling has spawned a plethora of issues. In the final analysis, most of these issues revolve around the concept of user access to information.

Traditionally, libraries in federal agencies, state agencies, municipalities, counties and academic institutions have been significant sources of information in the western culture. Major research libraries like the Bodleian (Oxford University), La Bibliotheque Nationale (Paris), the New York Public Library and the Library of Congress (Washington, D.C.) have operated as researchers' "gold mines." In the course of history, literary scholars, inventors, business executives, government employees, congressmen, students and professionals like accountants, lawyers or computer scientists have all resorted to such libraries as information sources. This does not necessarily mean that libraries are their only source of information. Nevertheless they have been and are still important sources.

With the advent of the commercial computer-based data banks, a lot of the information "business" is being eroded away from libraries. There may be a parallel between "fast food" chains versus elite restaurants and "fast information" banks versus libraries. Fast information banks do charge a commercial fee but usually deliver relevant information faster than libraries. Several libraries are buying services from data banks, although users may go directly to database vendors. Erosion of services has been accentuated by the emergence of independent information specialists—with titles varying from information brokers, through free-lance librarians to simply information consultants.[15] Such brokers act as intermediaries between the large data bank vendors and the end user and thus by-pass the library. By providing information on demand, they are very effective middlemen. The fees issue is essentially how to make computer-based data banks accessible to the library clientele and who should pick up the tab?

Having examined the information industry and market in Chapter 4, it is tempting to accept Susan Artandi's assertion that,

> We live in an information-rich world in which information is bought, sold, traded, exchanged and consumed in economic terms. It is treated both as a product and as a commodity to be used in the process of attaining human goals. As we are moving toward a post-industrial knowledge society, information is recognized more and more as a resource that can be developed, controlled, and utilized.[16]

In other words, in our age, information is in many respects a commercial commodity.

While this premise is becoming gradually obvious, the notion of charging fees for library services especially in publicly supported information sources raises emotionally charged reactions. Both sides for and against fees have plausible arguments which have been well articulated in the literature. Amidst the heated debate, however, certain facts surrounding the controversy are sometimes blurred.

Three aspects are particularly overlooked while discussing the issue, especially by critics who are against fees. In the first place, information is not really a free good. This may be looked at in two respects. First, the production and acquisition of information involve the expenditure of other resources.[17] Second, even in terms of a "free" library, where information should be provided free, the taxpayer will have paid for the service well in advance by way of property or other taxes.[18] In other words, the "freeness" of the information is a relative term, when compared to payment for a service or a good on a cash delivery basis.

Second, granted that libraries, especially public libraries are deemed public utilities, this is not sufficient reason to exempt them from user charges. Marilyn Gell[19] indicated that the public has been conditioned to paying for other public utilities like bridges and highways. This implies that they may be reconditioned to pay for some specialized services in libraries.

Thirdly, one of the aspects overlooked is the long history of charging fees for special library services even in public libraries. Commenting on this issue, Alan Kusler reminded us that, "Rental collections in public libraries are nothing new; many libraries have had them for several decades. Nor is the controversy over their just and proper role in the tax supported institutions new. Professional journals have been debating the issue in their pages since the 1870s."[20] In addition, library users have for a long time been subject to overdue fines, and fees loans of current best sellers and interlibrary loans.[21] Furthermore, photocopying, which was introduced into libraries in the 1930s,[22] has hitherto been charged to users with no apparent resistance.

If user fees have been known in libraries for decades, one would wonder why they have recently evoked heated debates. An attempt to answer this puzzle was made by DeGennaro who referred to the advent of relatively expensive computer-based bibliographic services.[23] As a result of these services, new outlooks and horizons are being unfolded on the information scene. For instance, deeper and speedier reference service for the user is facilitated. For example searching MEDLINE could indicate to a clinical doctor recent research on a given disease within minutes. Since these services are available in other fields of knowledge, information specialists who cannot provide them find themselves ineffective. In several instances, it is neither a question of jumping on the bandwagon, nor a luxury, but rather a matter of survival. On the other hand, library budgets have not kept up with either inflation or additional services. They face a dilemma which was aptly described by Cogswell when he said that, "The only real alternatives to charging fees appear to be to cut back still further on existing services or to discontinue online services altogether. Faced with choices such as these, the question to be answered will not be whether to charge but rather how much to charge for online searching."[24]

Advocates of fees, too, bear the blame in overlooking or exaggerating aspects of the problem. Among the most significant are first, self interest and second, the idea of a free public library. When Eugene Garfield[25] testifying before the National Commission on Libraries and Information Science (NCLIS) said that he disapproved of libraries competing with for-profit information centers, he was promoting vested interests. One would not have expected a president of a private information processing center or the chairman of the Information Industry Association to have aired a different opinion.

Another important aspect which is overlooked by fees advocates is the deeply ingrained tradition of the free library service, particularly in public libraries. One tends to believe DeGennaro when he says that "the idea of free public libraries is firmly embedded in the American tradition, and anyone who tries to undermine it will encounter fierce opposition."[26]

Careful scrutiny of the literature on the fees issue reveals a recurrence of arguments or points scored on either side. Some are significant and others facile.

Arguments Against Charging Fees for Information

Some of the significant points advanced include the following:

1. That the American tradition of free library services is damaged by charging fees.
2. Users are double charged, first by taxes for running public services and then by charges for special services.
3. Before one can charge one must have a sound basis for charging. It is argued that methods of evaluating information are still primitive.
4. Charging fees causes inequalities vis-à-vis the users, for only those who can pay may use special services. This negates the equal access to education ethic.
5. Acquisition of materials will begin to be geared to those who can pay.

Arguments for Charging Fees for Information

Equally justifiable points have been presented for fees as follows:

1. The tradition of selling services to those who can pay is part of the American culture.

2. Subscription libraries as well as rental collections are well known features in American library history.
3. Users pay for other public utilities like bridges, highways, museums and parks.
4. Fees will allow development of special services which would not otherwise be provided, like on-line bibliographic searches.
5. Users do not seriously object to charges for services which are vital to them.
6. If fees are not collected, some of the costly services would be abused and thus become a drain on the budget.

Observations from Some Libraries Charging Fees

A study made of four public libraries in Northern California under the name of DIALIB[27] showed that library patrons do accept user charges. As regards University libraries, Cogswell's[28] study at the University of Pennsylvania and Hitchingham's[29] study of several universities revealed that academic library users generally accepted user charges. They nevertheless revealed that students gave limited support to library fees. An M.I.T. study on the other hand, suggested that accessibility to "soft money" from grants may be an important factor in easy acceptance of fees.[30] Due to increasing cutbacks on library budgets, more academic libraries are investigating ways of cost recovery. According to some academic library administrators, the issue is no longer fee or free. It is rather How soon? How much? and How?[31]

Public Versus Private Provision of Information

Fee enthusiasts, particularly information brokers and database vendors, have gone beyond the basic fees issue. They have also posed the question of who should be the major provider of information during the Information Age. Largely due to the competition vendors face from government agencies providing similar information services, they have made several presentations against government provision of information. First, it is contended that the U.S. economy is built on the concept of free enterprise, which should be extended to the information business. Second, it is argued that entrepreneurial effort and competition will allow users to have more choice among services.[32] Consequently, quality services will result while the price is moderated. Thus, they submit that Uncle Sam must exit from the information business.

On the other side of the coin, Martha Williams[33] has pointed out that if the U.S. government had not carried out or sponsored much of the pioneering work in the development of databases and on-line systems, the information industry in the U.S. and worldwide would not have reached its present stage. Through government agencies like the National Science Foundation, National Aeronautical and Space Administration (NASA), the National Library of Medicine and the Armed Forces, the taxpayers' money was dished out as "seed money" for research and development. The taxpayer is thus entitled to subsidized information services accruing from this initial investment.

Other critics have pointed out that the public sector usually provides general types of information. There will always be groups of people with higher income and with a higher value of information than will be provided by the public sector.[34] Thus the competition will be different from the cut-throat business type envisioned by the Information Industry Association.

Professional rhetoric has so far not suggested standard solutions. Practical exigencies, however, dictate that cost-recovery arrangements be exercised whereby some of the cost is borne by the end user. Be that as it may, it must be recognized that with the best will in the world, some people may not be able to get the vital information they need. There is thus need for federal, state or city policy to rectify the issue of providing information to those who need it for survival and genuinely cannot afford to pay for it.

LEGAL PROBLEMS IN USER ACCESS TO INFORMATION

Legal problems pose another set of issues relevant to user access. Three topics are covered in this chapter: copyright, freedom of access to information and privacy. While cognizant of the magnitude of the issues, we attempt to give salient points vis-à-vis user access. In addition, we note the apparent contradictions when the topics are considered *in toto*; all one can say is "That is the nature of the beast!"

Copyright Law and User Access

Copyright law essentially protects the fruits of intellectual labor manifest in scientific or creative work. The 1976 Copyright Act[35] made comprehensive revisions to the U.S. copyright law based on the 1909 Copyright Act.

While the 1976 Act strengthened the right of copyright ownership and broadened the scope of what may be copyrighted, it also maintained easy access to copyrighted works. Prior to the 1976 Act, it was difficult to decide when a copyrighted work was being fairly utilized. Litigation of copyright infringement had hitherto had recourse to the doctrine of fair use developed by the judiciary. This doctrine was codified in Section 107 of the 1976 Act which gave the following guidelines for determining fair use:

> In determining whether the use made of a work in any particular case is a fair use the factors to be considered shall include
>
> (1) the purpose and character of the use, including whether such use is of a commercial nature or is for nonprofit educational purposes;
>
> (2) the nature of the copyrighted work;
>
> (3) the amount and substantiality of the portion used in relation to the copyrighted work as a whole; and
>
> (4) the effect of the use upon the potential market for or value of the copyrighted work.[36]

As for user access *per se*, Section 107 is the most significant part of the Act. Is access to electronically stored data or programs guaranteed by the 1976 Act? Part of the answer to this question is found in legal literature. Analysts have convincingly argued that although computer-based data banks or computer programs are not specifically mentioned, the category "literary work" as specified by the Act is broad enough to include them.[37] By the same token, the fair use doctrine can be equally applicable to information data banks. In other words, copyright law implicitly permits bona fide researchers to use copyrighted materials inclusive of electronically stored works.

Freedom of Access to Information

Federal and state freedom of information laws were enacted in the wake of the Vietnam era when public hearings attested to the need for such legislation. The 1966 Freedom of Information Act (FOIA), subsequently amended in 1974, was designed to make available to the public information possessed by the government within legitimate confines of secrecy.[38] This opened a flood of requests to what we have referred to as societal information systems.

In an attempt to pursue the principle of "open government" or the public's "right to know," freedom of information law created problems with regard to personal data. According to FOIA, each government agency must provide information on request within ten working days of the request.[39] Nine exemptions curtail wholesale access to all government records; in other words, access has somewhat been bridled. Exemption 6 concerning personnel files mentioned medical and similar records. It was partly because the FOIA exemptions did not go far enough that personal privacy became an issue in the 1970s.

Privacy Legislation

Public and congressional interest in privacy may be traced to fears conjured by nationwide data banks containing personal information. The Information Age has ushered in gigantic computer-based data banks of information on individuals. Federal and state agencies as well as private corporations, especially credit institutions, have billions of such records in their computerized data banks.

Political surveillance and wiretaps during the Nixon administration, creating events collectively known as "Watergate," accentuated public concern for privacy. However, the concept of personal privacy and its legal protection is not new. At the close of the nineteenth century, Samuel D. Warren and Louis D. Brandeis explored the principle of privacy in their article entitled "The Right to Privacy."[40] Their arguments have in the main been the foundation of current privacy law.

The Privacy Act of 1974 was in response to these concerns and aimed at defining individual rights by restricting government handling of personal information. The Act may be deemed to curtail "over access" to public information which happens to be personal records—on income, criminal records, scores on tests, and several other categories.

The amount of personal records kept in federal data banks is startling. According to Bacon and Kelly,[42] nearly 4 billion records on individuals are stored in federal data banks. For instance, the Department of Health and Human Services is reported to have 1.3 billion personal records on marital, financial, health, and other information for recipients of Social Security, social services, Medicare, and welfare benefits. Similarly, the

Treasury Department has over 853 million records for taxpayers, foreign travelers, persons deemed by the Secret Service to be potentially harmful to the president, and dealers in alcohol, firearms, and explosives.

Whereas there is legal provision for and general consensus on the need to protect these data banks, there is evidence that presently, personal information is not adequately protected against misuse. Investigators of the Social Security computer system found that it lacked tight security. Rooms housing data terminals were left unlocked at night and passwords to the system were bandied about by the agency's employees.[43]

Some of these lists are sold to private firms compiling mailing lists for product markets. For example, it is legitimate for the Detroit-based R.L. Polk & Co. to acquire records from a state motor vehicle registry. Such information may be matched with another government agency's list to generate a product marketing profile. Using consumer psychoanalytical techniques, such lists can be used by business corporations to manipulate consumption of certain products. According to the 1977 Privacy Protection Study Commission Report, "The rules that affect the mailing lists practices of government agencies at all levels are among the murkier areas of public law."[44]

Finally, the public and information professionals should still be concerned that the majority of corporate data banks which contain personal information are not covered by the 1974 Privacy Act. In contrast for Western Europe (Sweden, Norway, Denmark, West Germany, France, Austria, Iceland and Luxembourg)[45] personal information in private and public data banks is protected by law. It is important to note that while U.S. corporations may resent this protection at home, they willingly accept it in order to do business with European countries.

CONCLUSION

While we espouse ample user access to relevant information, we should not be misconstrued to subscribe to blatant exposure of private personal information. As we get gradually immersed in the Information Age, the value of information as a survival tool increases. The fees controversy centers around attempts to keep this "tool" available to a large portion of society. Admittedly information entrepreneurs have an important part to play. It is partly in response to the demand of individual entrepreneurs as well as information centers that Chapter 6 has been developed. Nevertheless, society should have an obligation to provide information to people who need it for survival but who cannot genuinely afford to pay for it.

Advocacy of user access, "open government" and the "right to know" impinges on copyright and personal privacy law. This does not constitute fundamental contradiction of principles. What society is basically saying is "Let us have controlled access to computer-based data banks we have so painfully and elaborately constructed for our convenience."

NOTES

1. Harold Leavit, *Managerial Psychology*, 4th ed. (Chicago: University of Chicago Press, 1978), pp. 65-71.

2. Philip E. Slater and Warren G. Bennis, "Democracy Is Inevitable," *Harvard Business Review* 42 (March-April 1964):54.

3. Patrick Wilson, *Public Knowledge, Private Ignorance* (Westport, Conn: Greenwood Press, 1977), pp. 57-61.

4. A. P. Garvin, *How to Win With Information or Lose Without It* (Washington, D.C.: Bermont Books, 1980), p. 15.

5. Andrew Wessel, *The Social Use of Information Ownership and Access* (New York, Wiley-Interscience, 1976), pp. 1-8.

6. *The White House Conference on Library and Information Services, Washington, D.C. 1979. Information for the 1980s* (Washington, D.C.: Government Printing Office, 1980), p. 17.

7. *The White House Conference*, p. 9.

8. A.H. Maslow, *Motivation and Personality* (New York: Harper, 1954), pp. 80-85.

9. Allen Newell and Herbert Simon, *Human Problem Solving* (Englewood Cliffs, N.J.: Prentice-Hall, 1972), p. 9.

10. Peter H. Lindsay and Donald A. Norman, *Human Information Processing*, 2nd ed. (New York: Academic Press, 1977), pp. 540-86.

11. T. D. Wilson, "On User Studies and Information Needs," *The Journal of Documentation* 37 (March 1981):5-10.

12. Susan Artandi, "Man, Information and Society: New Patterns of Interaction," *Journal of the American Society for Information Science* (January 1979):16-17.

13. James Oates, "Convention Theme: Levels of Interaction between Man and Information," *American Documentation* 19 (July 1968):290-91.

14. A. W. Pearson, "Problems of Information Transfer," *Aslib Proceedings* 25 (November 1973):415.

15. Lorig Maranjian and Richard Boss, *Fee-Based Information Services* (New York: R.R. Bowker Company, 1980), pp. 1-11.

16. Susan Artandi, "Man, Information and Society," p. 15.
17. *Ibid.*, p. 16.
18. Richard DeGennaro, "Pay Libraries and User Charges," *Library Journal* 100 (February 1975):366.
19. Marilyn Gell, "User Fees I: The Economic Argument," *Library Journal* 104 (January 1979):22.
20. Alan Kusler, "Rental Collection: Pro and Con," *Library Journal* 84 (June 1959):1753.
21. Marilyn Gell, "User Fees II: The Library Response," *Library Journal* 104 (January 1979): 19-23.
22. Richard DeGennaro, "Pay Libraries," p. 366.
23. *Ibid.*
24. James A. Cogswell, "On-line Search Services: Implications for Libraries and Library Users," *College and Research Libraries* 39 (July 1978):278.
25. "IIA Urges User Fees for Libraries in NCLIS Testimony," *American Libraries* 4 (June 1973):335.
26. Richard DeGennaro, "Pay Libraries," p. 366.
27. Roger Summit and Oscar Firschein, "Public Library Use of Online Bibliographic Retrieval Services: Experience in Four Public Libraries in Northern California," *Online* 1 (1977):60.
28. James Cogswell, "On-line Search," p. 278.
29. Eileen Hitchingham, "Use of Commercially Vended Online Data Bases by Academic Libraries," *ASIS Proceedings* 12 (1975):158-59.
30. Allan Benefeld, et al., "User Receptivity to Fees for Service Computer-Based Reference in a University Community," *ASIS Proceedings* 12 (1975):151-52.
31. Elizabeth Lunden, "The Library as a Business," *American Libraries* 13 (July-August 1982):471-72.
32. "Government vs. Private Sector in the Supply of Information," *Publishers Weekly* (May 5, 1975):28-29.
33. Martha E. Williams, "Highlights of the Online Database Field—1982." In *Proceedings of the National Online Meeting, 1981* (Medford, N.J.: Learned Information, Inc., 1981):2.
34. Christine Whitehead, "Pricing Information Services." In M. Raffin, *The Marketing of Information Services* (London: ASLIB, 1978), p. 19.
35. *Public Law 94-553*, October 19, 1976.
36. *Ibid.*, Section 107.
37. Louis P. Pataki, "Copyright Protection for Computer Programs Under the 1976 Copyright Act," *Indiana Law Journal* 52 (1977):504.
38. Kenneth A. Kovach, "A Retrospective Look at the Privacy and Freedom of Information Acts," *Labor Law Journal* (September 1976):548-64.
39. *Public Law 89-554*, September 1966, Section 6(A).

40. Samuel D. Warren and Louis D. Brandeis, "The Right to Privacy," *Harvard Law Review* 5 (December 15, 1890):193-220.

41. *Public Law 93-579*, December 31, 1974.

42. Donald C. Bacon and Orr Kelly, "Uncle Sam's Computer Has Got You," *U.S. News and World Report* 84 (April 10, 1978):44-48.

43. Susan Artandi, "Computers and the Post-Industrial Society: Symbiosis or Information Tyranny?" *Journal of the American Society for Information Science* 33 (September 1982):302-7.

44. *Personal Privacy in an Information Society. The Report of the Privacy Protection Study Commission, July 1977* (Washington, D.C.: U.S. Government Printing Office, 1977), p. 130.

45. Robert E. Smith, "Privacy Still Threatened," *Datamation* (September 1982):297-306.

6
Pricing Information Services and Products

A given price for a product or service is an offer or an experiment to test the pulse of the market. It attempts to answer the question "How much do you think people will pay for this item?"[1] Like all experiments, pricing is a dynamic function within the marketing field. It is thus very rare that prices are fixed for all time. Even with government intervention, where prices may be temporarily fixed, adjustments are usually made for inflation or other causes.

Economists and business analysts have, over the years, developed a profound body of knowledge for determining prices. It is normally referred to as the "price theory." Elaborate mathematical and econometric models exist to help us decide what price to charge and when to charge that price. In spite of the scholarly finesse with which these models have been analyzed, some scholars have questioned their practical applicability.

In this chapter, we attempt to give an overview of pricing principles with reference to information services and products. We have deliberately minimized the mathematical computations with the hope that in that way the concepts will be understood by a larger audience and subscribe to our doctrine of user access to information.

Much of the activity of the information industry and market discussed in Chapter 4 deals with business transactions based on pricing. Within the information business, pricing regular information products like hardware and software is relatively easy. A number of reasons may be advanced for this relative ease. First, most hardware producers are comparable to any other conventional business enterprises. In most cases, they have been in operation for a long time manufacturing information processing products. Second, like the automobile or furniture industries, it is possible to provide a fairly accurate estimate of how much direct material or direct labor has been utilized in manufacturing a computer terminal or a disk drive. Third, over the years statistics have been compiled which are used as input into statistical or mathematical pricing models. Finally, due to the large sizes of most of these enterprises, they have large numbers of research staff who have acquired expertise in pricing.

On the other hand, the Information Age is continuously spawning services which transcend the traditional information processing equipment manufacturing firm. Information services currently provided through information data banks, information brokers or some libraries do not fit into the conventional mold. For example, it is difficult to estimate how much direct labor or material has gone into a computer assisted market survey or a computer-based on-line literature search. Nevertheless, pricing principles can be used as guides.

Due to reductions in operating budgets information centers and libraries have had to institute charges for some of the computer-based services they offer. In addition, database producers and information brokers find themselves confronted with pricing decisions. Ploughing through the available literature reveals very little research of relevance to information services and products. Some consulting firms like King Research Inc.[2] have investigated differential pricing for database producers. They have, however, concentrated on how a producer may set prices for a hard copy, an on-line service and database tapes containing the same information.

Information professionals who venture into charging fees for products need more than the bare essentials of pricing methods. Price setting is a component of marketing and product design. Thus in order to see the price theory in perspective, it is necessary to understand at least the elementary principles of marketing. Librarians have toyed with the idea of getting FISCAL (Fee-based Information Service Centers in Academic Libraries)[3] or running a library as a business. If one decides to do "some" business in an information center or library, it is imperative to "get one's feet wet"—get acquainted with marketing principles of which pricing is a part and get a firm grasp on pricing alternatives.

PRICE THEORY

Stripped of its econometric models and mathematical embellishments, price theory, with reference to a given firm, corporation, information center or library, has three basic elements. First, what are the information center's objectives? This may depend on whether it is a nonprofit, not-for-profit, or an open profit-oriented enterprise. Second, what are the methodologies available for setting prices? These may include untested theoretical constructs. Finally, given the center's objectives and available pricing methods, how can these be implemented for a given situation? It is important to note that an individual center is a unique entity and theory must be visualized within the relevant environment of the center. That is what we refer to in our analysis as optimum pricing.

Pricing objectives may differ among firms even when they operate in identical business categories. Similarly, information centers or libraries may have different pricing goals. Five main objectives may be identified in setting a price. First, prices are set to achieve a target return on investment. Given a dollar value of investment in development of a service, the price may be set such that a specified percentage of profit will be made. Second, large companies or information centers may set prices to stabilize the price (the going rate) on the market. Presently, some large information centers like MEDLARS (Medical Literature Analysis and Retrieval System) based at the National Library of Medicine or Lockheed Information Retrieval System of Lockheed Corporation are capable of doing this. Third, prices may be set to improve or maintain the company's share of the market. Young firms or partnerships may set low prices to capture the buyers' attention. In that case initial profits may be minimal. Fourth, prices are set to meet or prevent competition. Finally, prices are set to maximize profits. In spite of public relations pronouncements to the contrary, most firms try to get as much profit as possible and commodities are priced accordingly.

As a component of the marketing concept, price theory has been amenable to quantification. Quantitative and graphic analyses have been used widely. Three main methods have been used as will be elaborated later. In the first place, there is the cost based pricing method. In this case, the price reflects what it cost the firm to acquire or develop the service plus a percentage profit. Secondly, there is the demand based pricing method, which involves varying the price according to the commodity's demand on the open market. Finally, there is the competition based pricing, depending on what the other operators are offering.

Awareness of the pricing methods or developing objectives leaves the firm with yet other pricing issues. These are centered around the characteristics of a given firm or information center and its relevant clients. A pricing strategy must be developed as the final process to decide whether the price will be place, time or client dependent, leading to price discrimination. In addition, strategy must include what types of discounts need be given and finally, how is the pricing system affected by government regulations and laws.

UNDERSTANDING MARKETING PRINCIPLES IN INFORMATION PRICING

As already intimated, pricing is a vital component of marketing. The activities of market operators described in Chapter 4 are indicative of the need to use marketing principles and practices in information handling. This is pertinent to purely commercial enterprises as well as nonprofit organizations, such as libraries and information processing centers. Benson Shapiro's comment in this report is worth noting when he said that,

> For years, certain successful marketing techniques that were once considered to belong almost exclusively to profit-motivated business enterprises have been used by alert managers in private non-profit organizations. However, many other managers of non-profit organizations have failed to recognize that marketing is as intrinsic to the non-profit sector as it is to the business community.[4]

Weinstock asserts that after two decades of solving theoretical, technical and production problems, it is imperative for the information service producer to become more knowledgeable about the marketing function.[5]

One of the key ideas in contemporary marketing for business enterprises is the "marketing concept." It was promulgated in the 1950s and centers around the notion of "user-orientation."[6] As Kotler[7] explained it was an alternative to two other concepts, product orientation and sales orientation. While the product orientation emphasizes the ways of increasing output of units for sale, the sales orientation concentrates on how sales will be increased to achieve high profits. On the other hand, the "marketing concept" stresses satisfying consumer needs as perceived by the various categories of consumers.[8]

In the case of library and information centers, user satisfaction should be the *sine qua non* of practitioners. While attempting to perfect ways of collecting and processing information, the information professional must work out ways of assessing user needs. Kuehl crystallized the primacy of the user when he said that, "A 'user orientation' means that the Information managers and scientists should attempt to define the *generic* product and service needs of user groups by looking *outward* toward the user as opposed to looking inward toward the product."[9] In other words, the marketing concept pervades all facets of society where goods and services are rendered. All types of information centers particularly those supported through government and other nonprofit institutions and societies ought to be capable of "selling themselves" (marketing) in order to (a) continue to survive in stringent budgetary situations and (b) serve user needs and demands as the user perceives them.[10] Inevitably, in setting a price for an information product or service, the marketing concept becomes relevant when the clients' interests are accounted for.

Several aspects pertaining to marketing can be adapted for information products. For instance, consumer behavior techniques developed in business situations could be relevant in information product design. In addition, sampling and data analysis methods should be examined for relevance.

"Market segmentation" discussed in Chapter 4, which aims at grouping the user "universe" into small, nearly homogeneous units to which effort may be directed, is significant in information pricing. It consists of a body of marketing thought and literature directed toward (a) defining and (b) measuring the needs of specific subgroups.

Another marketing technique which readily comes to mind is promotion. Some information centers, especially libraries, have been accused of playing a passive role, expecting the user to go to them, without necessarily being informed of their existence or location. The main purpose of promotional campaigns is to identify the information agency and its products and services and to acquaint the prospective user with the agency's records in meeting its commitments. In addition, they should introduce the agency's principal representatives.

Andrea Dragon[11] attempted to illustrate how some of the techniques may be used in libraries. She concluded that librarians can no longer assume that the public will continue to accept increases in taxation for the support of libraries with no promotional endeavors. Positive action using marketing techniques must be taken to attract the tax dollar. She continued that failure to recognize the need for such an approach will lead the library to lose to other competitors like high school marching bands and public golf courses.

This is not peculiar to nonprofit organizations, for some of the information brokers have had marketing problems too. One of the problems is caused by the novelty of an on-line search as a product-cum-service. Managers attempting to set prices have no precedents. In addition, because an on-line search contains information which is an intangible product, it *ipso facto* becomes difficult to attach an "equitable" price tag to it. Evidently, libraries and information centers in the United States are facing problems of inflation and reduced budgets. Whereas it is logistically enticing and operationally expedient to charge for some services, there appear to be no guidelines on how to arrive at "acceptable" or "reasonable" prices.[12]

Research done by the author in and around Pittsburgh (Pennsylvania) indicated that several libraries and information centers in both the private and public sector already charge for some information services. This was found common especially in those institutions purchasing information from commercial vendors like the New York Times Data Bank, Systems Development Corporation, Lockheed Information Retrieval Systems, Predicasts and Bibliographic Retrieval Services Inc. None of the libraries or information centers examined charged the end user a full economic price as would happen in the commercial market place. Almost all charged more than they were charged by the vendor whether private, like Systems Development Corporation, or government sponsored, like National Library of Medicine's MEDLINE.

As regards the final price, the basis for its calculation was invariably arbitrary. It varied from around 5 percent to 75 percent of the vendor's original price. Further questions about how they arrived at the various percentages were fruitless as apparently no rationale could be advanced. The most common response appeared to be that "our users have so far not complained about these charges."

Other than the tradition of a free library service, Weinstock[13] aptly suggests that one of the major problems of marketing information is the assessment of *value* contributed by products and services to parent organizations' effectiveness. Kotler, on the other hand, asserted that "the first thing an organization must decide in attempting to develop a price or pricing policy is the objective that it is trying to achieve."[14] Both Kotler[15] and Kuehl[16] see the profit motive as being ultimately applicable to private and public supported institutions. While the private sector stresses tangible profits, public agencies expect "abstract profit" to society. For instance, MEDLARS' profit is the provision of good health, while ERIC contributes to educational improvement for the American populace.

In spite of the problems of assessing the information worth, we shall examine the pricing mechanisms used in business management. Before discussing pricing methods, however, we briefly review cost concepts used in business.

Cost Concepts

Fixed Cost is an expression applied to elements such as executive salaries, rent, or property tax. It remains constant regardless of the quantity of units produced.

Total Fixed Cost refers to the sum of all fixed costs in a production process.

Variable Cost refers to elements such as material or labor which are directly related to the product. Variable costs vary with the volume of production. At zero production, the variable cost is also zero.

Total Variable Cost connotes the sum of all variable costs. The higher the volume of production, the higher the total variable cost and vice versa.

Average Variable Cost refers to the total variable cost divided by the quantity of units produced. Normally it decreases with the higher volumes of production; i.e., it varies inversely with the level of production.

Total Cost refers to the sum of total fixed cost and total variable cost for a given quantity produced.

Average Total Cost refers to the total cost divided by the quantity of units produced.

Marginal Cost refers to the cost of producing one more unit or last unit produced.

It is important to be aware of these standard definitions when fixing prices. Several administrators of information centers or libraries sometimes refer to cost recovery as an equitable price assessment practice. One would ask Which cost?

Cost Based Pricing

Use of a cost based pricing mechanism entails setting prices mainly on the basis of cost of producing the items. In retail enterprises it results in mark-up or cost-plus methods. This in effect implies adding some fixed percentage to the unit cost of production. Two defects of the scheme have been isolated. In the first place, the demand for the product is not taken into account in the final calculation. Secondly, undue confidence is placed in information on how much it costs to produce a given product.

Most organizations in the nonprofit sector cannot expect to find a price which would cover their cost. Even if acceptable formulas were devised, such prices would undermine the social benefits initially intended. Thus, the principle of "cost recovery" is used by several nonprofit organizations, with the ultimate result of recovering a "reasonable" amount of their total cost.

In most cases, cost recovery implies recovery of the fee the on-line database vendor charged the information center. It thus excludes staff time and implicit overheads like maintenance services, lighting and rent. In short, the center passes the vendor charges directly to the user.

As a corollary to the cost based methodology, the break-even point somewhat relates to cost recovery as perceived by center administrators. Break-even point is defined as the quantity of output (units produced) at which sales revenue equals the total cost at a given price. Put in another way, revenue equals the cost incurred. Table 5 shows how the break-even point is computed given hypothesized production cost statistics. Figure 12 shows the break-even point at a price of $50 per unit and Figure 13 illustrates break-even points at four different prices. Two assumptions are made in these statistics. First, variable costs are assumed constant at $20 per unit cost of output. Second, total fixed costs are constant at $300. Stated as a simple algebraic expression

$$Y = \frac{TFC}{P - AVC}$$

A Unit Price	B Unit Variable Costs	C Contribution to Overhead (A − B)	D Overhead (Total Fixed Costs)	E Break-even Point (D ÷ C)
$	$	$	$	Units
30	20	10	300	30
40	20	20	300	15
50	20	30	300	10
70	20	50	300	6

Table 5. Break-Even Point Computation

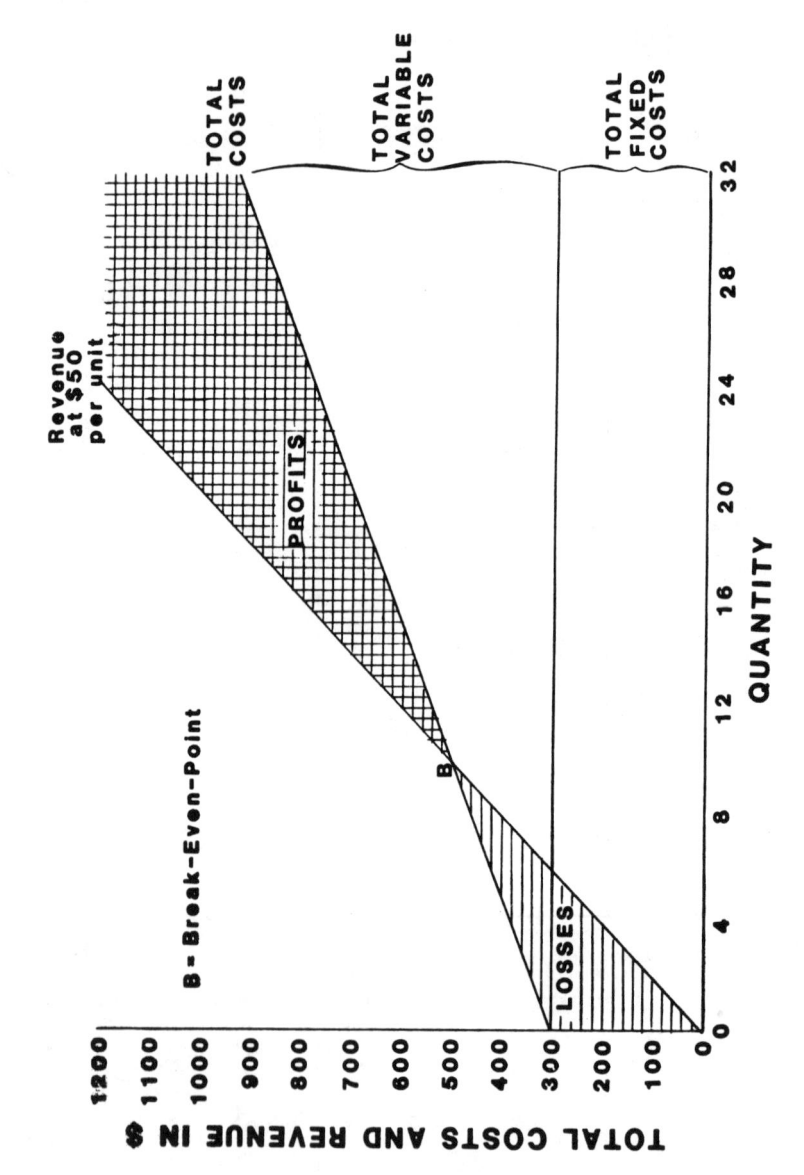

Figure 12. Break-Even Point at $50 Per Unit

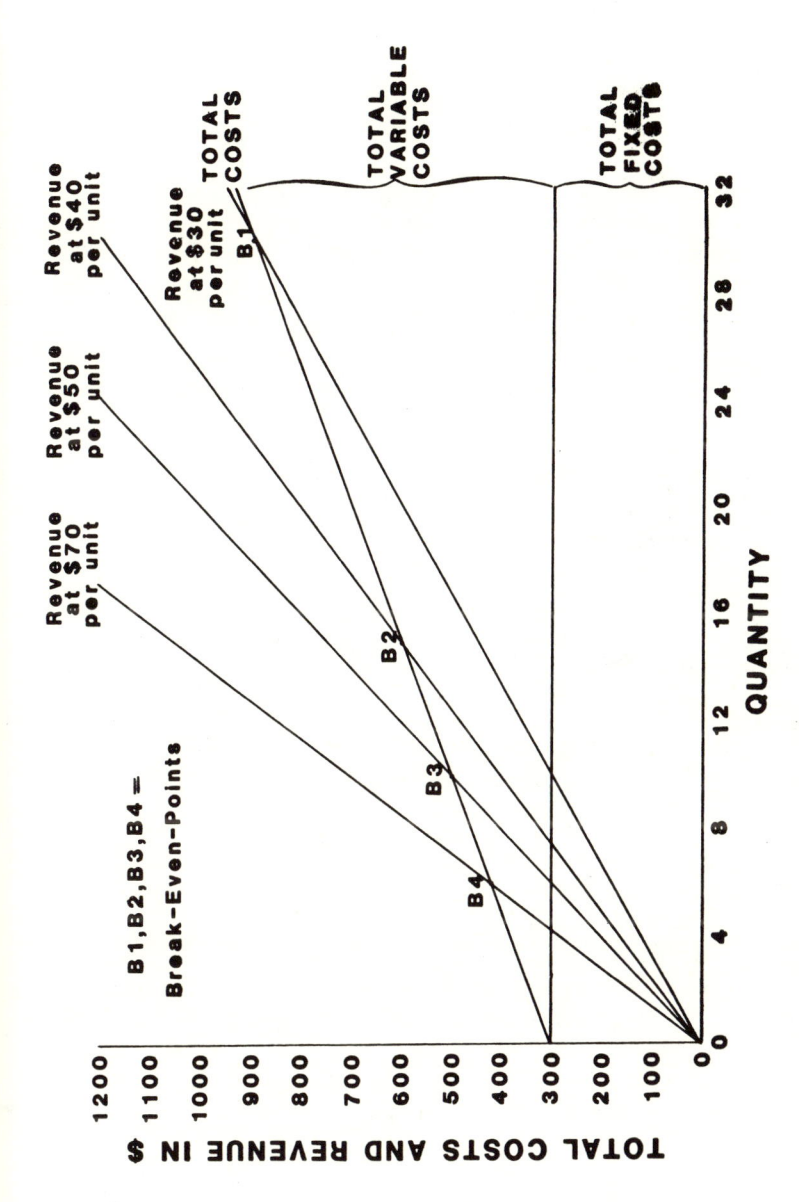

Figure 13. Break-Even Points at Four Different Prices

where: Y = Break-even Point
TFC = Total Fixed Cost
P = Selling Price
AVC = Average Variable Cost

As an aid to pricing, the break-even point analysis indicates how many units must be sold at a given price to recover the basic costs. However, it does not indicate whether that particular quantity can be sold on the open market. Furthermore, it suffers the general cost-based problem of providing precise cost statistics as previously defined.

Demand Based Pricing

Demand based pricing may be used. It concerns looking at the intensity of demand for a product or service. The higher the demand the higher the price. While this approach might be valid, it disregards the *value* of information.

Critics of the supply and demand analysis also contend that accurate data is usually not available to make the analysis and set a price. It may be used to study past performance and indicate trends but is not very accurate for immediate price definition.

Competition Based Pricing

Competition based pricing may be relatively easy to adopt, as it depends on other institutions' prices. The "going rate" is followed by whoever is in the industry. This may be popular in library and information centers where the costs are difficult to measure. In this case, the going rate price is equivalent to the collective wisdom of the industry about a price which would yield a fair return. Conforming is also felt to lead to harmony within the industry.

A number of criticisms have been made to competition based pricing. First, unless the industry is closely knit, the "going rate" may be illusory. The question arises as to who announces the "going rate." Second, it disregards the demand for the product. Finally, it may be based on a large firm's market leadership, and smaller firms with lesser economies of scale may be trading at minimal or no profits.

Optimum Pricing

Optimum pricing concerns keeping the specific firm, information center, library or information broker's specific needs in mind. Relations with clients may be a factor. Thus, a pricing strategy must be developed to work out the finer details.

Relations with various types of clients or customers result in price differentials. First, there is the practice of discounts, which may be based on quantity or cash/credit purchase terms. Second, there may be price differentials among customers due to geographic locations.

The various discount methods result in different prices for different customers. Caution must be taken against infringement of anti-trust laws which regulate interstate commerce. The Robinson-Patman Act of 1936 prohibits price discrimination in certain circumstances. It prohibits differential pricing *if it can be shown* that the practice is injurious to fair competition.

While discussing the possible adoption of these pricing techniques, Zais warns that

> Flexibility be maintained when approaching the issue of pricing information services and products. There are many models of pricing behavior that can be explored for their applicability... To create successful pricing policies, management needs a knowledge of the organization's costs and some knowledge of the market in which the organization operates. Research is needed to learn who purchases information services and products and their sensibility to price. More purposeful cost data gathering is needed—not only efforts to improve accounting data or historic cost data but also research that takes up such issues as joint costs, avoidable costs, and correct allocation of overhead.[17]

In the non-profit sector of the information arena, it may not be sufficient to consider the various pricing alternatives, for one is always saddled with the public interest centered around the tax dollar.

NOTES

1. William Stanton, *Fundamentals of Marketing* (New York: McGraw-Hill, 1981), pp. 221-79.

2. Donald W. King, "An Approach to Pricing Bibliographic Data Products and Services." In *Information Interaction, Proceedings of the 45th ASIS Annual*

Meeting, 1982 (Washington, D.C.: American Society for Information Science, 1982), pp. 149-50.

3. Elizabeth Lunden, "The Library as a Business," *American Libraries* (July-August 1982), pp. 471-72.

4. Benson D. Shapiro, "Marketing for Nonprofit Organizations," *Harvard Business Review* 51 (September-October 1973):123.

5. M. Weinstock, "Marketing Scientific and Technical Information Service." In *Encyclopedia of Library and Information Science*, vol. 17 (New York: Marcel Dekker, 1976), p. 166.

6. J. B. McKitterick, "What Is the Marketing Management Concept?" In Frank M. Boss, ed., *The Frontiers of Marketing Thought and Science* (Chicago: American Marketing Association, 1957), pp. 71-81.

7. Philip Kotler, *Marketing for Nonprofit Organizations* (Englewood Cliffs, N.J.: Prentice-Hall, 1975), pp. 43-53.

8. Edward W. Cundiff, *Fundamentals of Modern Marketing* (Englewood Cliffs, N.J.: Prentice-Hall, 1976), pp. 22-37.

9. Philip G. Kuehl, "Marketing Perspectives for ERIClike Information Systems," *Journal of the American Society for Information Science* 23 (November-December 1972):326.

10. *Ibid.*

11. Andrea C. Dragon, "Marketing the Library," *Wilson Library Bulletin* 53 (March 1979):498-502.

12. Harriet W. Zais, "Economic Modeling: An Aid to the Pricing of Information Services," *Journal of the American Society for Information Science* 28 (March 1977):89-90.

13. Weinstock, "Marketing Scientific and Technical," p. 165.

14. Kotler, "Marketing for Nonprofit," p. 178.

15. *Ibid.*

16. Kuehl, "Marketing Perspectives," pp. 361-62.

17. Zais, "Economic Modeling," p. 95.

7
The Management of Information Resources

One of the dominant issues of the Information Age is the management of information resources. The development and proliferation of different types of information processing technologies has rendered the traditional data processing organizational framework obsolete.[1] In Chapter 2, we discussed the concept of "compunication" whereby communication systems can compute and computer systems can communicate data. In addition to computer and communication networks, some of the technologies which have expanded the information processing function include word processing, library technology, computer based reprography and robotics. Consequently, the organizational structure whereby most institutional information processing was under the data processing department must be redesigned.

The key word is productivity. Business and national economy analysts have often stressed the primacy of information technology in improvement of productivity. William Norris asserted that "superior microelectronics and computer technology provide the critical basis for competitive advantages in other industries."[2] Other than the technologies, the quality of information used in decision making must be carefully monitored. While we do not subscribe to Connell's views regarding information as a "non resource," we accept his notion about it as a "brain food" that is "the feedstock used in the intellectual process of managing other resources."[3] Information technology as well as the information product must be managed for productivity.[4]

In our approach, we define the management of information resources as the marshaling and coordinating of information resources to achieve institutional objectives. Three broad activities may be identified in the information resources management function. First, human resources deployment, which involves effective utilization of information expertise. Second, material resources allocation, involving the effective utilization of data processing or communication equipment. Finally, information product quality control, to ensure that high quality information is used in decision making for optimum productivity.

THE PROBLEM

In the 1960s and 1970s, the data processing departments in large institutions enjoyed supremacy as the centers of information processing. This was partly demonstrated in the power of the DP "manager" in selection of data processing equipment and size of his or her budget vis-à-vis total expenditure on information processing. The computer center, as it existed then, serviced the needs of the accounting, personnel, marketing and other departments. This central position prevailed in academic institutions, business corporations, federal, state, and local governments. In some institutions, especially business corporations, the DP manager controlled and was responsible for 80 percent of total information processing expenditure.[5] In addition, he or she had the ultimate approving authority for expensive equipment.

Technological developments in the late 1970s and 1980s have, however, changed the role of the DP manager and his department. As Figure 14 indicates, new information technologies have outgrown the conventional data processing environment. As a result, the head of data processing is gradually losing most of his power. In the first place, some of the technologies need extra skills which are not usually found in a traditional data processing department. For instance, although computer based, data communications is associated more with telecommunications than data processing, word processing is allied to secretarial skills, CAD/CAM systems are associated with engineering design, and library technology is more akin to library user needs. Secondly, the DP manager no longer controls a lion's share of information-processing funds. Finally, ultimate approval for capital expenditure on information-processing equipment may be vested in the initiating divisions or departments. These tendencies are both inevitable and desirable, for they allow initiative and resourcefulness to be maximized in units where the technologies are developing.

But, in spite of the benefits of initiative encouragement, the technologies as well as the information processed must be effectively coordinated. Business corporations have to manage these two sectors of the information function for productivity, while nonprofit organizations manage them for effectiveness. In their research on the information needs of national, state and local organizations, McGowan and Loveless[6] strongly stressed the need for strategic planning and management of information in the public sector. In other words, the private sector (business corporations) as well as the public sector (universities, federal, state and local agencies) need to coordinate the technologies to achieve institutional objectives.

INSTITUTIONAL INFORMATION NETWORK COMPONENTS

A conceptual network as depicted in Figure 15 may develop as a result of technological growth in information processing. As mentioned earlier, the technologies have a computer base, although their specific functions in the organization may differ. A consequent scenario is described in subsequent paragraphs.

The data processing unit carries on the conventional duties of statistical analysis, number crunching and information storage and retrieval. Closely connected to data processing is the telecommunications or data communications unit which receives and communicates data originating from the other institutional units. In addition, it acts as the receiving and communication port for external information agencies.

The computer-based reprographics unit would include computer output on microfilm (COM), facsimile productions, and interactive graphics. There are links with data communications and data processing, for some of the data reproduced will have originated from these units.

Office automation, according to current literature, contains virtually anything imaginable. Such elements as word processors, teleconferencing, and audio/video equipment like recorders and dictaphones that are connected to computers would constitute the unit.

Within the information network, the computer based information center or library would have a master on-line catalog. Such a catalog would be accessible from an office, a home or a classroom with remote terminals to see if the library has a given item. In addition, it would be used to see if the item is actually out on loan to another library user.

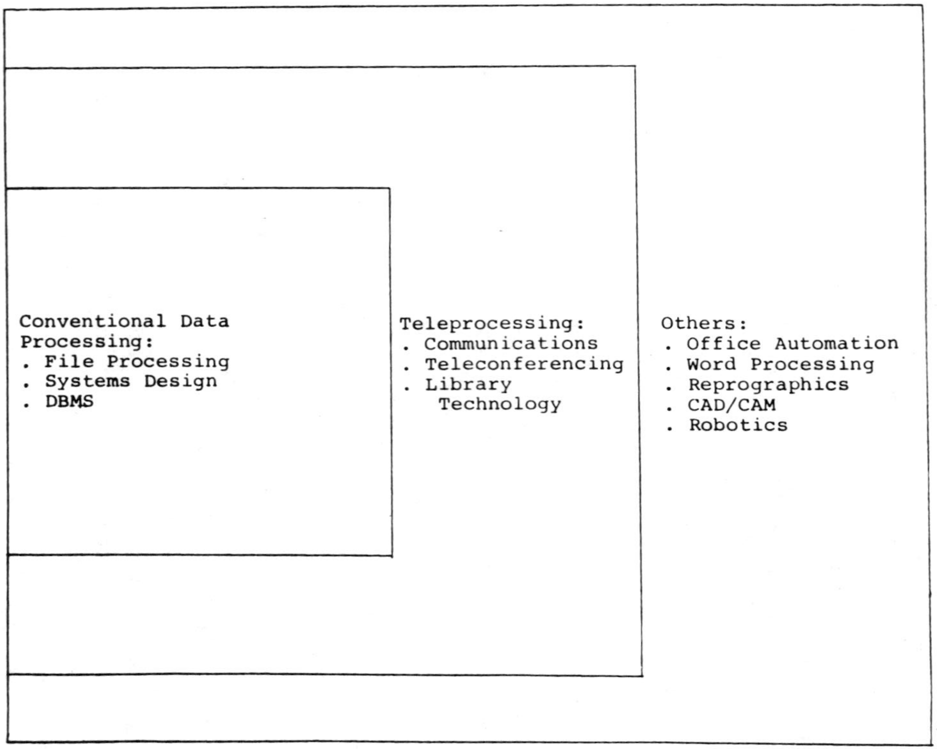

Conventional Data
Processing:
. File Processing
. Systems Design
. DBMS

Teleprocessing:
. Communications
. Teleconferencing
. Library
  Technology

Others:
. Office Automation
. Word Processing
. Reprographics
. CAD/CAM
. Robotics

Figure 14. Information Technologies Growth Progression

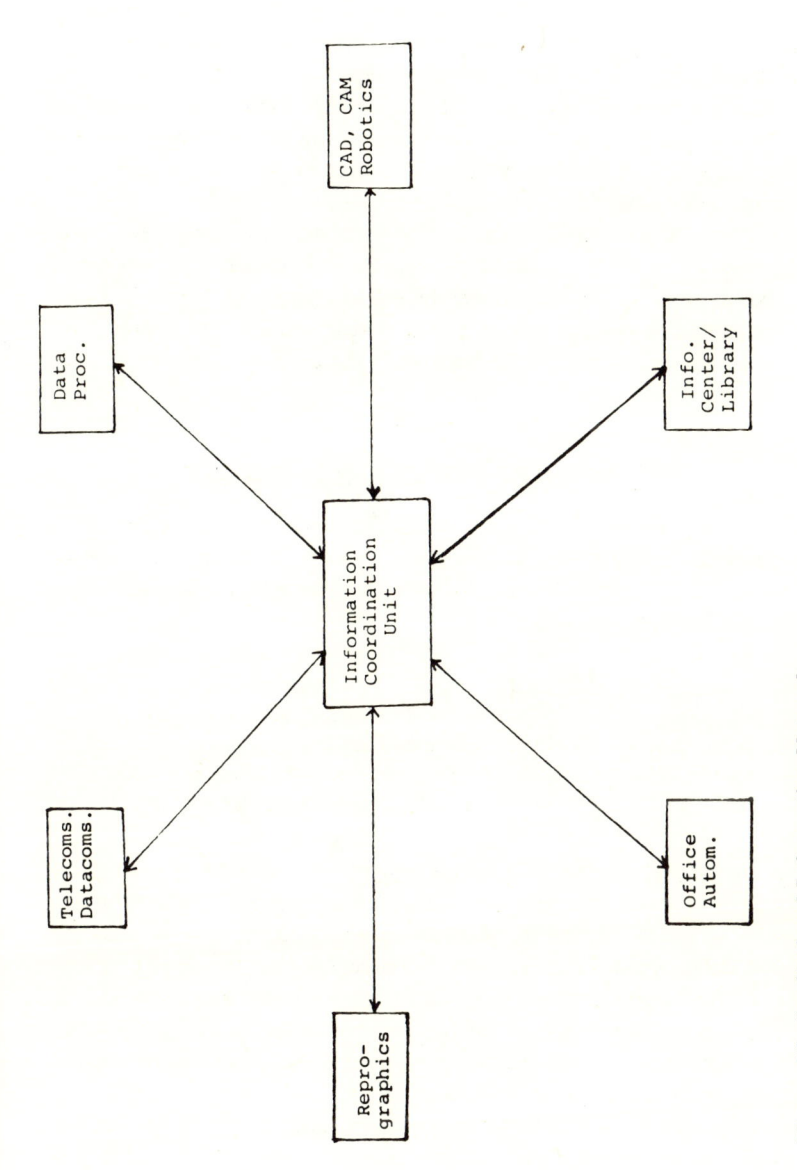

Figure 15. Institutional Information Network

The U.S. Library of Congress SCORPIO system is typical of a prototype on-line catalog which large information centers would have in the 1980s. In addition to local bibliographical sources, the computerized information center would access other distant data centers for material exchange, purchase or loan purposes. Thus as an information storage and retrieval center, the library becomes a major computer and data communications utilization unit of the organization.

Finally the CAD/CAM and robotics unit may initially be peculiar to business corporations. On the other hand, it is conceivable that robotlike devices will, in due course, be used by large public organizations for simple chores like issuing tickets. Already banking institutions have automatic tellers and the technology is currently available to produce animated tellers.

IN SEARCH OF COORDINATION

The importance of accurate, timely information cannot be overemphasized for the 1980s. It is needless to add that information must be effectively processed. Murray's prophesy reflected the Information Age trends when he asserted that

> "winners" of tomorrow will be those corporations that can react quickly in a rapidly changing environment. It takes a great effort to acquire the fleetness of foot needed to organize information in a structure which will meet user needs and an infrastructure which will allow ready access across divisional and departmental boundaries—indeed, across continents.[7]

Strategic planning for information resource management is needed not only for business corporations, but also for nonprofit organizations.[8]

Several reasons may be advanced for the need for strategic planning and coordination of information resources. In the first place, there is need for quality control of the information an organization needs for decision making. We have already referred to the adage "garbage in, garbage out" to symbolize the problem caused by poor quality initial data used in information processing.

Secondly, there is need for standardizing master records. Institutions which need to use common records have developed central data banks. Some of these banks are manipulated using database management systems (DBMS). In a DBMS environment, there is a standard record which may be accessed by various service points. For example in an academic institution, there is a student record which is used by the accounts department for tuition payment verification, the library for overdue books, and the registrar's office for academic records. Similarly, in an insurance corporation, a client's record can be used for various purposes in the organization. Coordination is needed in such an environment to determine who authorizes changes in the master record. In addition, privacy restrictions under the Privacy Act dictate that only a certain specified category of operators may examine personal records. Policy must thus be developed with regard to record handling. In other words, the creation of data banks involves policy initiation, development, implementation, and cross checks, all of which must be carefully coordinated.

Thirdly, economies of scale are realized in mass production. In spite of the dispersed information processing units, some functions would be cheaper if performed in a central spot. For instance, a centralized ordering department would reduce the clerical staff needed at the individual units. Furthermore, it would result in reduction of costs rendered by quantity discounts on purchases. Another area where economies of scale would be realized is printing. Cost of printing large jobs may be reduced when centralized. Quality and speed will also be improved by using say high speed laser printers. Inevitably, such activities would need coordination.

Finally, coordination of units is vital in eliminating unnecessary duplication of activities or services. In some organizations utilizing services from commercial data banks, the central administration may purchase data communications services from TELENET, the technical library may use AT&T and the medical center may use TYMNET when accessing the same data banks! In such a situation, wastage of funds can be avoided by initiating a central data communications policy and minimizing the number of data communications vendors.

CRITICAL MANAGEMENT FUNCTIONS

Having discussed the rationale for coordination, it is pertinent to identify the functions which call for management. Six main functions have been identified. First, there is need for long-term policy initiation and planning. As all the units are jointly attempting to achieve organizational objectives, broad policy directives should be given to guide unit managers. Such directives would be used as points of reference for unit managers' self-appraisal.

Second, there is need for restructuring the organizational framework. Some analysts discuss organizational structure as if the only modes available are dichotomous—centralized or decentralized. It is often forgotten that a hybrid system is also feasible whereby some information activities are centralized while others are decentralized. The concept of distributed processing which involves processing some of the jobs at the dispersed units is getting implemented in large organizations. The management function needed involves deciding what new units to create as well as the allocation of functions among the various units.

Third, there is the human resources allocation function. Within large organizations exist a large variety of information professionals. The information coordination unit (see Figure 15) in collaboration with the institution's personnel department should periodically review personnel competencies and ensure that there is effective utilization of available expertise. There is perennial criticism of computer scientists' lack of public relations and managerial skills. The coordinating unit should suggest to the personnel department ways of developing those skills on the job. Personnel who are willing to go through the "mill" should be encouraged to take formal MBA or MPA degrees or attend seminars and short courses. There are several conferences which are held in the U.S. throughout the year. The nature of information technology is such that new developments are announced at these meetings. As part of personnel development liberal funding must be provided for conference attendance. With these considerations, the coordinating unit must have a system-wide personnel policy.

Fourth, there is the material resources allocation function. This involves decisions on which equipment to acquire, where to locate it in the system, and who should be in charge of it. One of the regular duties of the coordinating unit is the equitable allocation of system active operating time. While the precise scheduling may be left to the unit manager's discretion the percentages of usage to be allocated to the institution's production and service departments must be done by the coordinating unit. For example how much computer or data communications time must the library have, or how much is to be used for the marketing, accounting, and personnel departments must be decided by the central coordinating unit. Inevitably, departments using information resources must be adequately represented at the central authority.

Fifth, there is the network performance evaluation function. The rationale for network existence is the provision of high quality information used in decision making. In academic institutions, the information technologies would enhance the students' learning process as well as supporting faculty teaching and research. As regards business enterprises, the network should provide appropriate information to enable the organization to achieve high productivity and meet competition from other corporations. A number of evaluative questions which may be posed periodically may include: Is the network as an entity effectively carrying out its mission? Are the component units performing at optimum levels? How does our network compare with other organizations? Assuming the funds are available, are we utilizing the latest or most effective techniques? For effective evaluation, it is desirable to establish performance standards by which the units may be evaluated.

Finally, there is need to take care of the crisis management function.[9] One of the ways to develop this function is to ask and attempt to answer "what if's." Several techniques may be used. Brain-storming, which is a group dynamics technique involving spontaneous generation of ideas, may elicit some of the "what if's" and the relevant responses. Comprehensive and constant literature search may be used to find how other institutions in similar situations have reacted. Establishing contacts with similar institutions may also reveal useful information. Lastly, additional information can be procured from consultants in information processing, who may furnish probable solutions.

MANAGEMENT STYLE

Current literature is fraught with suggestions on how to manage the disparate information technologies. Nolan suggests that management by committee is best.[10] On the other hand, Horton[11] advances the notion of a vigilant information manager who would challenge unwarranted expenditure on equipment or services by production and service departments.

While arguments for management of information technologies by committee are plausible, asserting that it is the categorical "best" is dangerously presumptuous. It is assumed that committee operations would be effective regardless of the size of the organization, the sophistication and differentiation of the component units and the prevailing organizational culture (is it Theory X, Theory Y or Theory Z type?).

We contend that choice of an appropriate management style is context and time dependent.

It is persuasive to resort to management theories and relate them to information technologies. Theories X and Y were promulgated by Douglas McGregor in his book *The Human Side of Enterprise*,[12] where he analyzed managerial assumptions about human nature. On the other hand, Theory Z is a pragmatic adaptive theory developed by William Ouchi[13] and aimed at selective adoption of Japanese managerial techniques to American organizations.

Admittedly management theories may be dismissed as abstract constructs which may not be relevant in specific situations. However, examination of some of the theories helps to clarify the thought process needed in developing management styles for information technologies. At professional conferences and in literature a common question often posed is "How shall we *control* the new information technologies?" The emphasis on control is essentially a Theory X approach to management, whereby authority is exerted through a bureaucratic hierarchy. Given the level of professional expertise and technical detail demanded by these technologies, one wonders whether the appropriate question should not rather be "How shall we *coordinate* the new technologies?" which is a Theory Y oriented question.

It is important to note that while we discuss management of information resources a lot of emphasis needs to be focused on "people management," as Ouchi aptly asserted:

> As a nation, we [United States] have developed a sense of the value of technology and of scientific approach to it, but we have meanwhile taken people for granted....Productivity, I believe, is a problem of social organization or, in business terms, managerial organization. Productivity is a problem that can be worked out through coordinating individual efforts in a productive manner and of giving employees the incentives to do so by taking a cooperative, long-range view.[14]

According to Theory X, the management assumes that workers are lazy and often dishonest. Workers lack ambition and must thus be controlled or prodded to work harder to achieve organizational objectives. The researches of McGregor and other industrial psychologists suggest, however, that these assumptions are not true in all cases. McGregor argues that the "carrot and stick" theory of motivation which accompanies Theory X does not work especially with high technology personnel. Theory X might be effective in a mass production conveyor belt working environment, where job specifications can be precisely predetermined. On the other hand, employees in high technology fields sometimes operate at the fringes of knowledge and precise job specifications may not be applicable. Consequently, Theory X which implies strict control must be replaced by other theories.

As for Theory Y, management sees employees as mature adults who have a built-in desire to exert themselves and contribute to organizational objectives. Workers can be creative and resourceful given a liberal working environment. Thus management encourages employees to exercise creativity and demonstrate responsibility by allowing them to think independently.

Finally, Theory Z is Ouchi's analysis geared to pragmatic selective adoption and adaptation of Japanese managerial techniques. Theory Z organizations are characterized by:

1. Lifetime Employment
2. Slow Evaluation and Promotion
3. Non-Specialized Career Paths
4. Implicit Control Mechanisms
5. Collective Decision Making
6. Collective Responsibility
7. Wholistic Concern

Ouchi stresses the fact that while not all these characteristics can be attained in the western world some have been associated with successful high technology organizations like IBM, Hewlett-Packard, the U.S. military and Eastman Kodak.

The relevance of these theories to the management of information resources lies in the emphasis which should be put on human factors. High technology is no more than the collective effort of the individuals who design and operate the component units. While the formal organizational structures might look like Figures 16 and 17, the vice president for information services should preside over a steering committee composed of unit managers plus production and service departments representatives. In large academic institutions, government agencies (federal, state, and local) and nonprofit organizations, the titles might be different, but the structure would resemble the model depicted. While

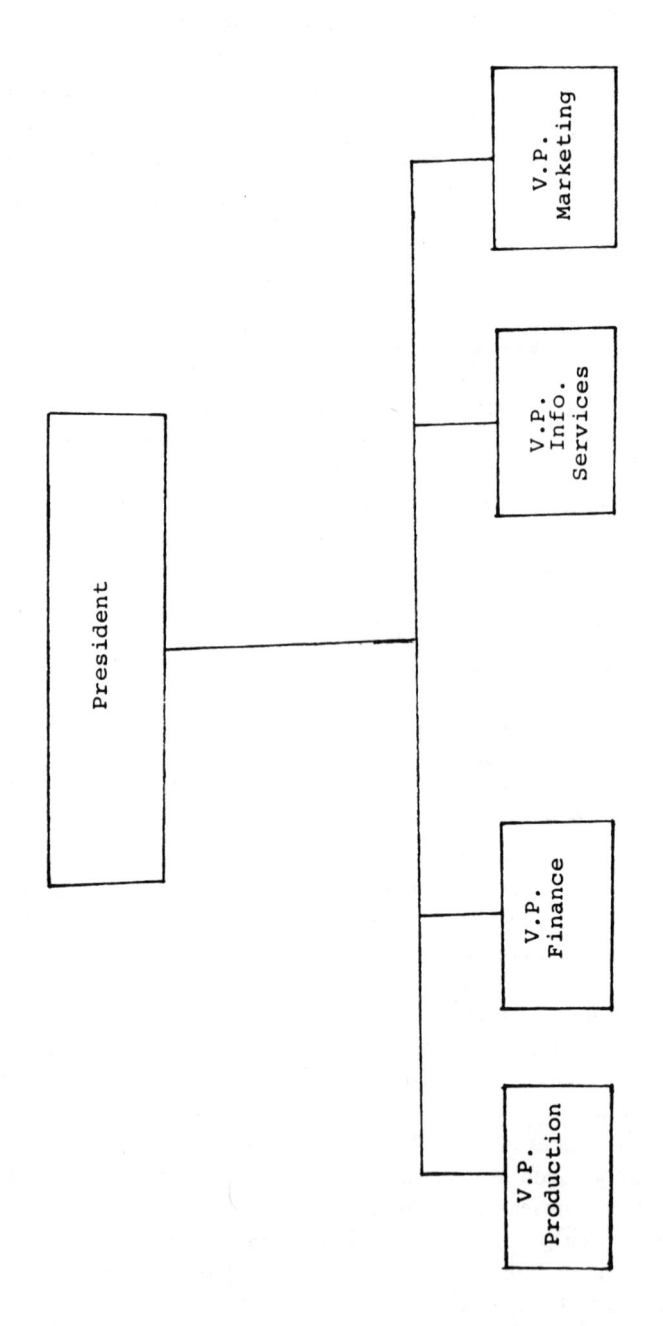

Figure 16. Simplified Corporation Organization Chart

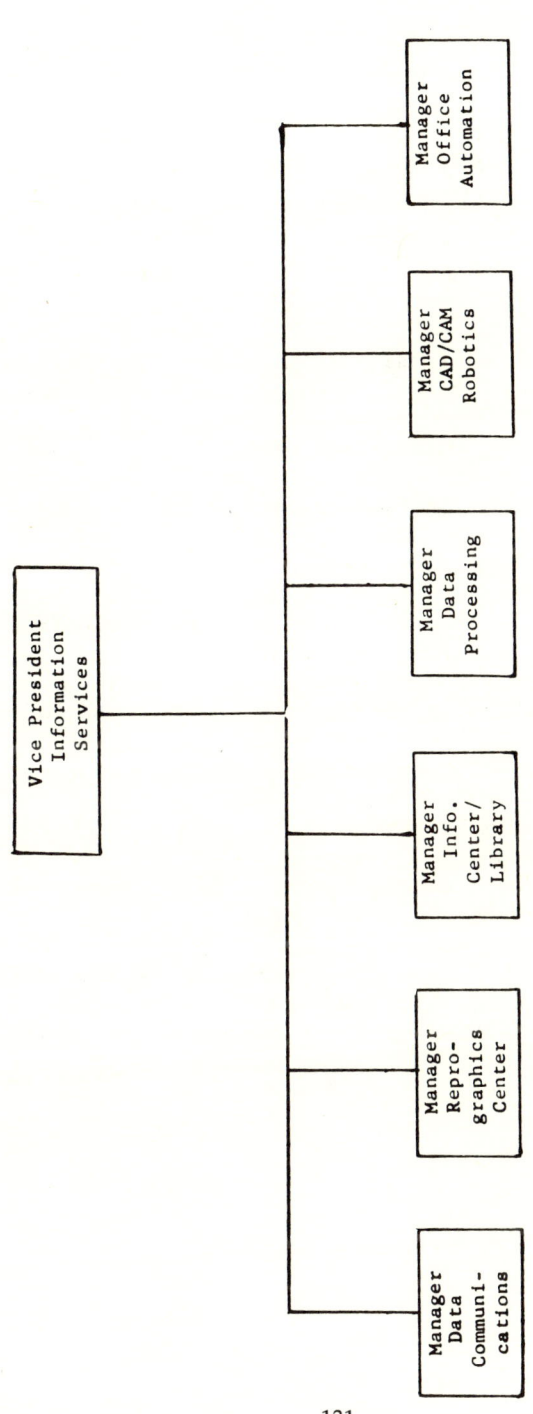

Figure 17. Information Services Division Organization Chart

decision making is a collective effort, the ultimate responsibility would be vested in the V.P. information services. In other words, high technology management would require application of both Theory Y and Theory Z.

NOTES

1. James L. McKenney and F. Warren McFarlan, "The Information Archipelago—Maps and Bridges," *Harvard Business Review* 60 (September-October, 1982):109-19.

2. William Norris, "Keeping America First," *Datamation* 28 (September, 1982):280-87.

3. John J. Connell, "The Fallacy of Information Resource Management," *Infosystems* 28 (May 1981):78-84.

4. Robert M. Ranftl, "Productivity—A Critical Challenge of the 1980s," *Infosystems* 26 (October 1979):55-66.

5. Richard Nolan, "Managing Information Systems by Committee," *Harvard Business Review* 60 (July-August 1982):73.

6. Robert P. McGowan and Stephen Loveless, "Strategies for Information Management: The Administrator's Perspective," *Public Administrative Review* 41 (May/June 1981):331-38.

7. Robert Murray, "Infosystems Opportunities in the 1980s Start with Management," *Infosystems* 26 (October 1979):119-20.

8. William R. Synnott, "Strategic Planning for Information Management Effectiveness," *Infosystems* 26 (October 1979):70-82.

9. Richard Nolan, "Managing the Crises in Data Processing," *Harvard Business Review* 57 (March-April, 1979):115-26.

10. Nolan, "Managing Information Systems," pp. 72-75.

11. Forest Woody Horton, Jr., "Information Management Czardom or Stardom?" *Information and Records Management* 15 (July 1981):14, 50, 51.

12. Douglas McGregor, *The Human Side of Enterprise* (New York: McGraw Hill, 1960), pp. 33-157.

13. William G. Ouchi, *Theory Z: How American Business Can Meet the Japanese Challenge* (Reading, Mass.: Addison-Wesley, 1981), pp. 1-94.

14. *Ibid.*, pp. 4-5.

8
Information Marketing Research

Information marketing research is a significant component of the streams of issues and activities propelled by information technological development. Whereas the management of information resources discussed in Chapter 7 coordinates information resources in an organization, marketing research asks questions and attempts to provide relevant information for information technology related decisions.

We define information marketing as the processes which include the design, promotion and distribution of information products and services to satisfy users' information needs. In other words, information marketing should be regarded as the link between institutions which have information goods and services to offer and clients with information needs and demands to satisfy. Information marketing research is thus the data collection and analysis component of information marketing.

Current trends indicate that during the Information Age, the primacy of information technology as the driving force for other business and governmental activities will be deeply entrenched. The introduction of new information services and products in organizations is already causing ripples and in some cases storms in office operations, manufacturing techniques, library practices and other society activities. Managers are faced with essentially marketing questions when deciding to introduce or continue computer-based information services or products. Some of the common questions include: What are the characteristics of our client groups(s)? How will our clients react to the new computer-based service? What are the competing services already existing on the market? Who are our main competitors? What is the probable consumption (sales volumes-units dispensed) for a given period(s)? What are the probable profits (losses or degree of subsidy for public services)?

All these are marketing research questions concerning the environment in which the organization is operating. Marketing research links an organization with its market environment. It concerns the identification, collection, analysis and interpretation of relevant information to help management tackle information technology oriented problems. Admittedly, the approach or techniques needed might be similar or even identical to those used for other problems. However, information seeking behaviors are different from behaviors caused by desire to acquire tangible products. As Aaker and Day[1] pointed out the marketing research activity in general is invaluable to both the private and the public sectors. Information marketing research is likewise vital in private and public organizations.

Information science literature has numerous examples of user studies which appear to be rudiments of marketing research. Three main criticisms have been leveled against most of these studies. First, they lack rigorous statistical analyses which similar studies in business have been subjected to. Second, they lack clear statements of achievable objectives. Finally, they lack logical connection with strategic planning activities of the organizations that might utilize them. In short, linkage is often not provided to allow practitioners to modify, adapt and possibly adopt the research findings.

This chapter attempts to give an overview of the information marketing research process. It gives examples of marketing research effort for computer-based information services. We start with home computer services and end with the Pittsburgh study. The last part tries to respond to the problem of what to charge or not to charge for computer-based services. Inevitably some of the concepts explored in Chapter 5 on user access recur in this chapter as research questions.

MARKETING RESEARCH PROCEDURE

When an organization is faced with client oriented decisions, say, in relation to introduction of a computer-based service or product, it may use available marketing research findings as the basis for various marketing strategies. Most organizational goals and objectives are unique and existing information may not be adequate. An institution may thus utilize an internal research team to work on a fact-finding marketing research project. Alternatively, an outside agency, usually a consulting firm with information technology expertise, may be hired to carry out the project.

While the procedure may differ from project to project the following are the major steps for any project:

1. Problem definition.
2. Discussion and clarification of the purpose of the research project.
3. Identification of objectives.
4. Design of the research study.
5. Conduct of the research.
6. Analysis and interpretation of the data.
7. Preparation of a written report for management.

As shown in Figure 18, these steps are connected chronologically until the research is concluded. The left portion of the figure depicts the constant use of the institutional information network as a source of research data. It is the same network concept developed in Chapter 6. For small organizations, the network may not be adequate for informational needs and researchers may resort to outside public information sources.

Problem definition involves getting acquainted with the organization and its conventional operations. In some texts, this is referred to as a situation analysis. After a thorough grasp of organizational operations, researchers zero in on the specific problem at hand, and analyze the main issues. In addition, hypotheses should be generated to facilitate clarity of the thought process. A hypothesis is a tentative statement of a probable answer to a research question. For example, it may be hypothesized that there is no difference in acceptance of personal business computers between engineering and humanities graduates. During the conduct of research, it may be shown that there is no relationship between type of professional training and desire to use or acceptance of personal business computers.

What is the purpose of the marketing research? After a clear problem definition, the purpose of the research gets clearer especially for sponsored research. In some instances, however, managers may have vague concepts which are not delineated until researchers ask further prying questions to discover the underlying rationale.

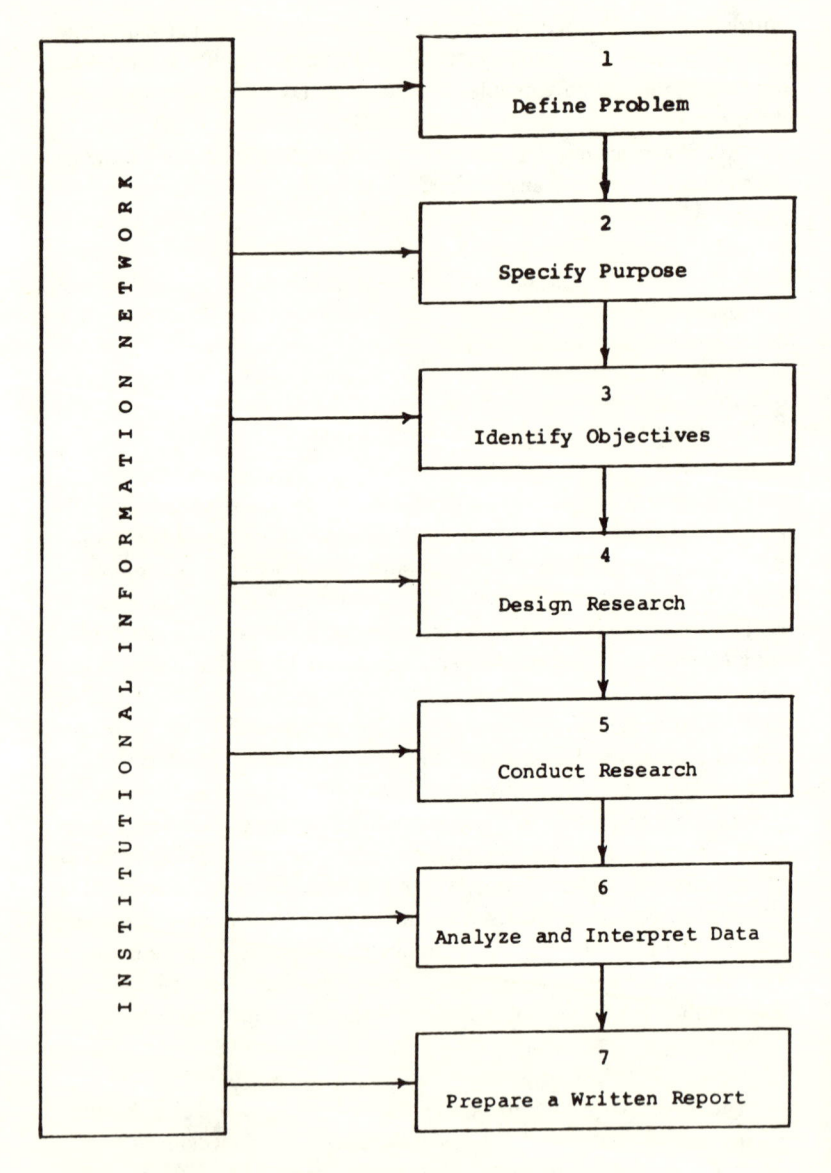

```
                                    ┌─────────────────────┐
                                    │         1           │
                              ┌────▶│   Define Problem    │
                              │     └─────────────────────┘
                              │                │
                              │                ▼
┌──────────────┐              │     ┌─────────────────────┐
│              │              │     │         2           │
│              │─────────────▶│     │   Specify Purpose   │
│              │              │     └─────────────────────┘
│  I          │                               │
│  N  I       │                               ▼
│  S  N  N    │              ┌─────────────────────┐
│  T  F  E    │              │         3           │
│  I  O  T   │─────────────▶│  Identify Objectives │
│  T  R  W    │              └─────────────────────┘
│  U  M  O    │                        │
│  T  A  R    │                        ▼
│  I  T  K    │              ┌─────────────────────┐
│  O  I       │              │         4           │
│  N  O       │─────────────▶│   Design Research   │
│  A  N       │              └─────────────────────┘
│  L          │                        │
│              │                        ▼
│              │              ┌─────────────────────┐
│              │              │         5           │
│              │─────────────▶│   Conduct Research  │
│              │              └─────────────────────┘
│              │                        │
│              │                        ▼
│              │              ┌──────────────────────────┐
│              │              │           6              │
│              │─────────────▶│ Analyze and Interpret Data│
│              │              └──────────────────────────┘
│              │                        │
│              │                        ▼
│              │              ┌──────────────────────────┐
│              │              │           7              │
│              │─────────────▶│ Prepare a Written Report │
└──────────────┘              └──────────────────────────┘
```

Figure 18. Marketing Research Procedure

For sponsored marketing research, discussion with management is vital in isolating specific objectives. Whereas unsponsored marketing research might appear too general to a cursory observer, business oriented marketing research anticipates what organizations might need for internal decision strategies. In some instances consulting firms compile marketing research packages in response to the felt needs expressed through contacts with decision makers or trade and professional associations. Thus, whether sponsored or not, a marketing research package should specify the objectives of the research effort.

Designing the research project taxes the researchers' expertise. It is at this stage when one decides which is the most appropriate methodology for data collection. Depending on the merits of the project, selection of approach may be between a survey and an experiment. If a survey is chosen, the next question is what will be the predominant method—mail, telephone, or interview. Another important consideration is the method of sampling—random, stratified, or restricted. General guides are available on research design, and the researcher's job is to select and design a suitable design.

Conducting the research is the implementation portion of the research design effort. Given the nature of the research problem, the researcher may emphasize primary or secondary materials. Primary data is the original data collected specifically for the research at hand. On the other hand, secondary data is that data which is reported in other sources—periodicals, reports or encyclopedias—which may be relevant for the research.

Finally, analysis of data is currently facilitated by ready made computer applications. Statistical packages have been developed for mainframe, mini and microcomputers to make detailed analyses feasible. In addition, packages abound on various types of report generation and representation. Soon after data has been collected, graphic transformations by computer—bar graphs, line graphs, three dimensional figures and pie charts—can now be generated in a very short time.

CASES IN INFORMATION MARKETING RESEARCH

Several studies have been done on computer-based products and services with regard to marketing issues. A small selection is examined to portray the issues that might recur in similar products or services marketing research activities.

Home Computer Services

In 1980-1981, Payment Systems Inc.,[3] an Atlanta based consulting firm, conducted a marketing research survey in the U.S. on home terminal services. One of its main objectives was to ascertain what segment of the U.S. population own home computers and what services they would be interested in accessing using home microcomputers or remote intelligent terminals.

Among the services often cited by respondents were:

1. Travel (airline, bus, etc.) reservations.
2. Weather reports.
3. Hotel bookings.
4. Banking—Electronic fund transfer (EFT), payment of regular bills.
5. Electronic mail—(messaging, terminal-to-terminal, batch or on-line).
6. Library inquiries—with direct connection to an online catalog or to an information bank.

Although this was a general marketing research report, it has been used as a reference tool by banking executives in planning long-range EFT systems. Data communications corporations have also used it to evaluate what data may be communicated to home computer units. Whereas data bank vendors consult it, many information center or library managers are not aware of its existence! The increasing use of home computers will in due course result in a demand to access on-line library catalogs via home terminals. The relevance of this report is that when managers of information centers and libraries are considering introducing on-line catalogs, ability to access such catalogs from domestic terminals should be part of the scheme. The report provides relevant data for such considerations.

Computer-Based Services in Public Libraries

The DIALIB project as it is often referred to in literature was sponsored by the National Science Foundation (NSF) between 1974-1977. It covered four public libraries in the San Francisco Bay area of California:

Redwood City Public Library, San Jose Public Library, Santa Clara County Library and San Mateo County Library. Computer-based search services using Lockheed DIALOG data bank were introduced in these libraries on an experimental basis.

It was a typical information marketing research project focusing on a wide range of practical problems. One of the main issues highlighted was the question of how the introduction of fees for library services affects the staff time and costs to the library providing the fees.

According to the project findings, "The time and cost required to perform a task in the free period was always higher than in the pay period."[4] To understand these conclusions, one has to consult the original reports and make some interpolations. Its significance lies in the fact that it set out to investigate information technological related problems using information marketing research techniques.

Computer-Based Services in University Libraries

Massachusetts Institute of Technology (MIT) libraries conducted an experiment in 1973-75 on computer based reference services they offered to their clients. It was funded by the National Science Foundation as part of the Northeast Academic Science Information Center (NASIC). A variety of databases available through Systems Development Corporation (SDC), Lockheed Information Retrieval Services and the National Library of Medicine's MEDLINE were offered.

Its main objective was to assess user receptivity to computer-based information services. A questionnaire was sent out to users and results were analyzed. According to the research findings, "over 80 percent of users were favorably disposed to the quality and cost effectiveness of the service."[5] Whereas most users readily accepted payment of fees, most faculty, staff, and graduate student researchers had access to "soft money" for research purposes. Like the DIALIB project, the NASIC/MIT study was a typical information marketing research project which provided decision makers with information on specific issues.

THE PITTSBURGH STUDY

The Pittsburgh (Pennsylvania) based study was conducted by the author in 1978-79 using institutions around Pittsburgh. More details are given on this study for two reasons. First, it covered a wider scope than either the MIT or the DIALIB projects. Second, it was a prototype opinion survey which may be replicated for information marketing research studies of similar issues. It compared and contrasted computer-based and manual search services. It was a user oriented project covering academic library users, users of corporation information centers and users of public libraries.

The problem researched was acceptance of fees particularly in publicly funded information centers or libraries. The introduction of relatively expensive computer based services made managers of information centers hesitate to charge or not to charge for these services. By seeking user opinions, the study attempted to gauge the clients' reactions. The following hypotheses were researched:

1. User charges are a deterrent to potential patrons of information services.
2. Industrial-based information users accept user fees more readily than academic or public library users.
3. Computerized bibliographical searches are more acceptable as regards fees than comprehensive manual literature searches or interlibrary loans.

The purpose of the study was to attract user involvement in the problem discussion. Professional rhetoric discussed in Chapter 5 seldom asked users' opinions about the fees issue. In more precise terms, the study aimed at:

1. Making a statistical analysis to see if there is any significant difference in attitudes towards fees among academic library users, public library users and industrial library users.
2. Making a statistical analysis to find out as to which of the three services are more acceptable for charging fees:
   a. Computerized bibliographical searches
   b. Comprehensive manual literature searches
   c. Interlibrary loans

As the research was user oriented, the main source of analytical data had to be the user of information centers and libraries. It was decided that for expediency, only users of public libraries, academic libraries and industrial libraries or information centers would be investigated. The research design was composed of a mail questionnaire (Appendix A) as the main instrument. A Likert-type instrument with five points

Institution	Conditional Acceptance	Unconditional Acceptance
Aliquippa Public Library		X
Carnegie-Mellon University		X
Northlands Public Library		X
PPG, Fiber Glass	X	
Western Psychiatric Institute and Clinic	X	
Westinghouse Electric Corporation - Nuclear Center	X	
Westinghouse Electric Corporation - Research and Development	X	

Table 6. Final List of Participating Institutions

and six sections numbered A-F was devised. It was supplemented by both telephone and personal interviews.

With regard to the selection of the research sample, strict random sampling was impossible to achieve. Alternatively a method referred to by Kerlinger as *purposive sampling* was used. As Kerlinger explained, "It is characterized by the use of judgment and deliberate effort to obtain representative samples by including presumably typical areas or groups in the sample."[6] Using this method, a number of institutions as shown in Table 6 were selected to provide the pool of respondents for the study sample. Unconditional and conditional acceptance connote unrestricted and restricted access to relevant institutional records, respectively.

Sample Characteristics

Sample characteristics are displayed by bar graphs. Throughout the chapter, Academic (abbreviated ACA) stands for academic library users,

Industrial (abbreviated IND) stands for industrial library user, and Public (abbreviated PUB) stands for public library users.

Area of Speciality

As shown in Figure 19, the largest subgroup was formed by scientists who amounted to 53.5% of the sample. This was followed by 23.6% of the "not applicable" category, followed by 15.7% social scientists and 7.1% humanities.

Status

There was a concentration of representation of research workers, who formed 37% of the whole sample (Figure 20). The "not applicable" category representing the "general user" is substantially represented, while other categories are well spread in the sample distribution.

Participation in a Funded Project

Figure 21 indicates that a large proportion of the sample, 61.4% have at some stage participated in funded projects. Among the projects implied are those originating from grants and those sponsored by federal or other agencies.

Previous Use of Computer Search Services

Figure 22 depicts proportions of exposure and nonexposure to computerized literature searches; 64.6% had used such services before as contrasted to 35.4% non users. Perhaps this might be expected in a sample with a large number of scientists.

Fee Deterrence

Figure 23 depicts responses to Question 37 (see Appendix A). The question was meant to determine whether charging fees was an important factor in deterring potential users from use of computerized services. Taking the group of respondents analyzed, 84.1% indicated that fees were not the main deterrent, whereas 15.9% said they were.

Sex

As shown in Figure 24, a large proportion of the sample was male, forming 66.1%. This was also reflected in the Academic and Industrial

Area of Speciality

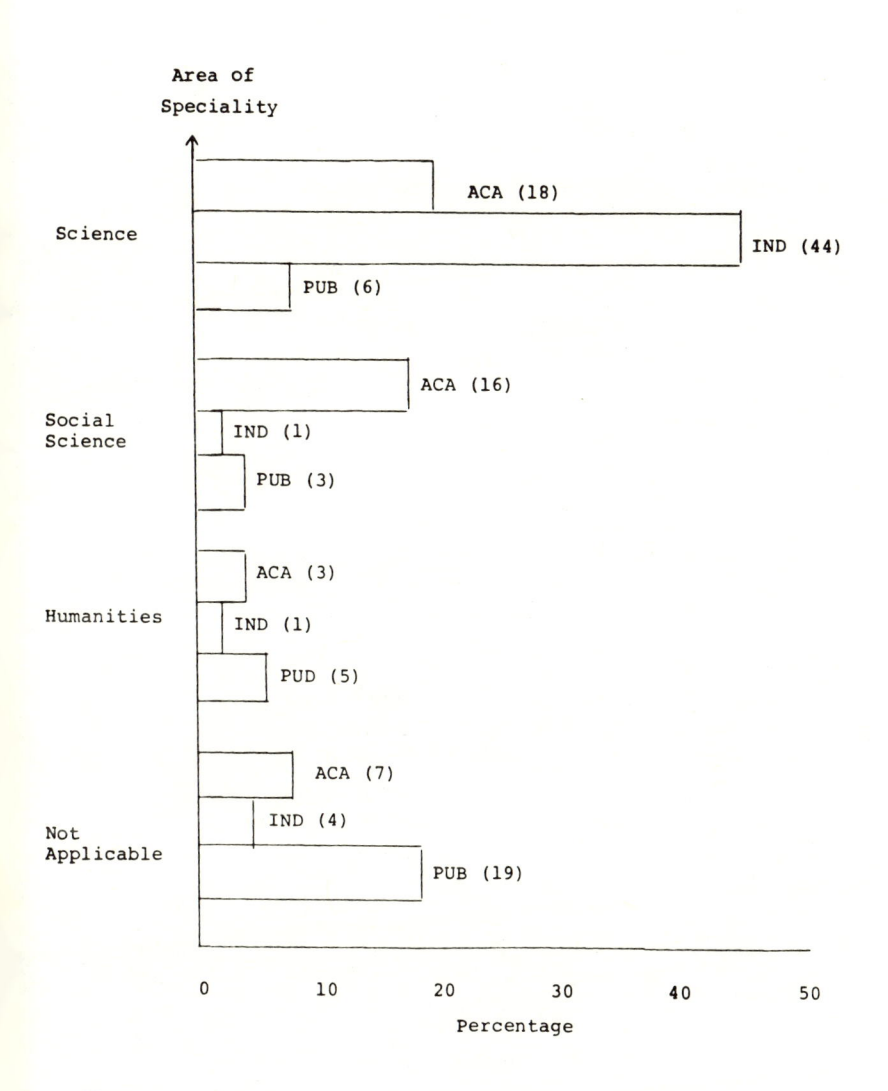

Science
- ACA (18)
- IND (44)
- PUB (6)

Social Science
- ACA (16)
- IND (1)
- PUB (3)

Humanities
- ACA (3)
- IND (1)
- PUD (5)

Not Applicable
- ACA (7)
- IND (4)
- PUB (19)

Percentage: 0, 10, 20, 30, 40, 50

Figure 19. A Histogram of Sample Distribution by Area of Specialty

Status

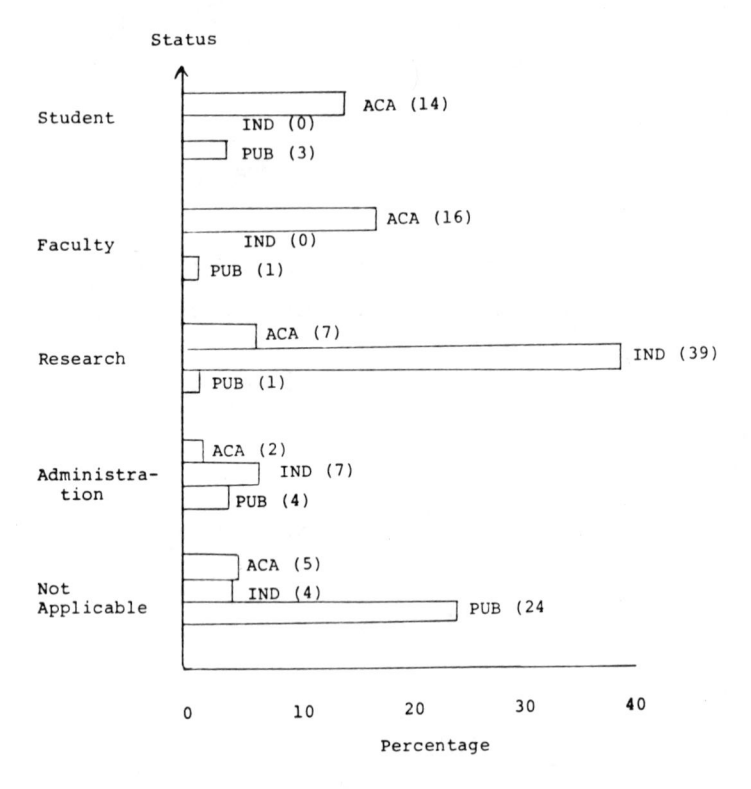

```
Student:     ACA (14), IND (0), PUB (3)
Faculty:     ACA (16), IND (0), PUB (1)
Research:    ACA (7), IND (39), PUB (1)
Administration: ACA (2), IND (7), PUB (4)
Not Applicable: ACA (5), IND (4), PUB (24)
```

Percentage

Figure 20. A Histogram of Sample Distribution by Status

subsets. However, the public library users subgroup had more female than male respondents.

Age

Figure 25 indicates a fair distribution in the sample with regard to age. A slight concentration was manifested between 30-49 which is reflected in standard library use figures.

Marital Status

According to Figure 26, a large proportion of the sample was married users. The married subset formed 76% of the whole sample. It was also proportionately higher in all the three categories; namely, academic, industrial and public library users.

Nature of
Participation

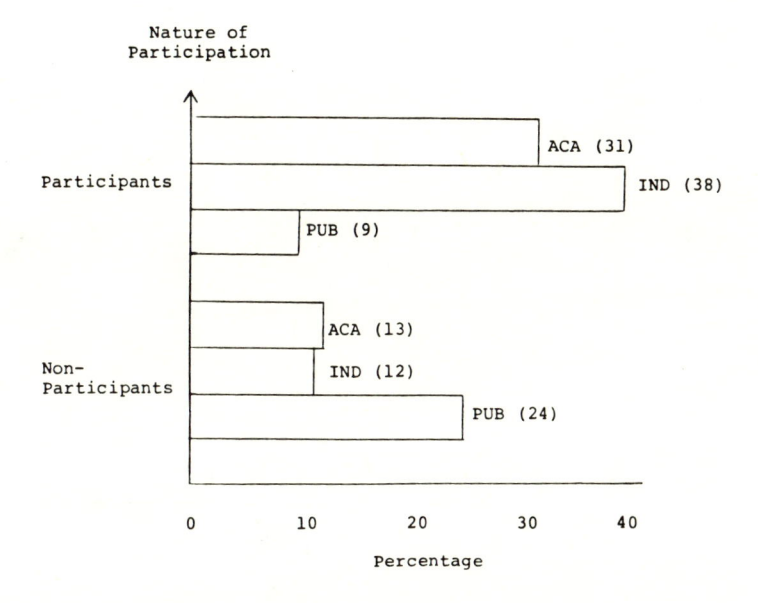

Figure 21. A Histogram of Sample Distribution by Participation in a Funded Project

Education

Figure 27 shows the breakdown by education. The sample distribution demonstrated a well educated group, with a large number of Ph.D. holders, 40.2%, and college non-Ph.D., 47.2%, the rest being largely high school or less. This is a fair representation of users of libraries as shown by user studies.

Income

Most people completed the request for the annual salary. As shown by Figure 28, a large number of respondents in the sample were in the $20,000+ income bracket. As an index of class of user, this demonstrates a concentration in the middle class category of society. Discussions in professional literature indicate that these figures relate to other studies about library users.

Prior Use

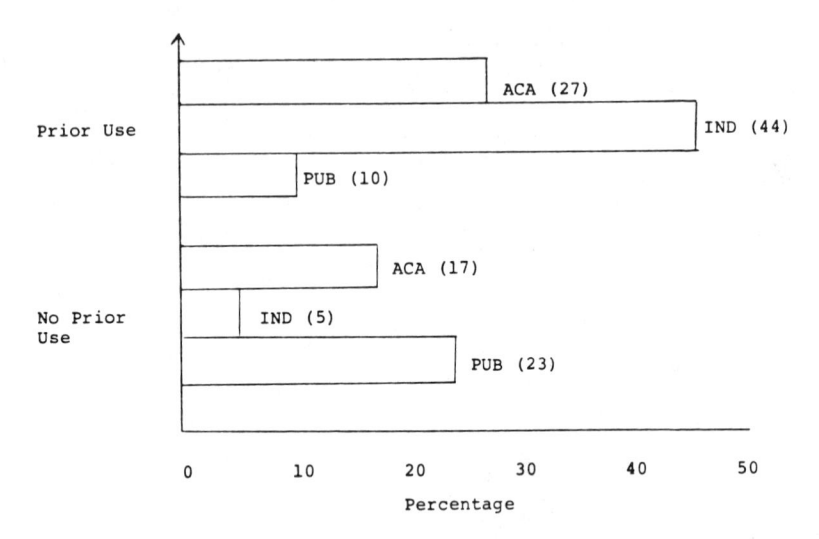

```
Prior Use      ┤ ACA (27)
               ┤ IND (44)
               ┤ PUB (10)

No Prior Use   ┤ ACA (17)
               ┤ IND (5)
               ┤ PUB (23)

         0   10   20   30   40   50
              Percentage
```

Figure 22. A Histogram of Sample Distribution by Previous Use of Computer Search Services

Data Analysis

Fees as a Deterrent

Section A on the questionnaire (see Appendix A) attempted to test the general question. Are fees a deterrent to potential patrons of information services? According to the figures in Tables 7 & 8 the sample did not have particularly strong feelings toward fees as a deterrent. All the three subgroups' means were around 3.0, which is the indeterminate figure.

Acceptance of Fees by Groups in the Sample

One of the major hypotheses which this study attempted to test was that industrial-based information users accept user fees more readily than academic or public library users. As acceptance depends on what service one examines, user responses were examined vis-à-vis the services covered in the study (see Tables 9–11).

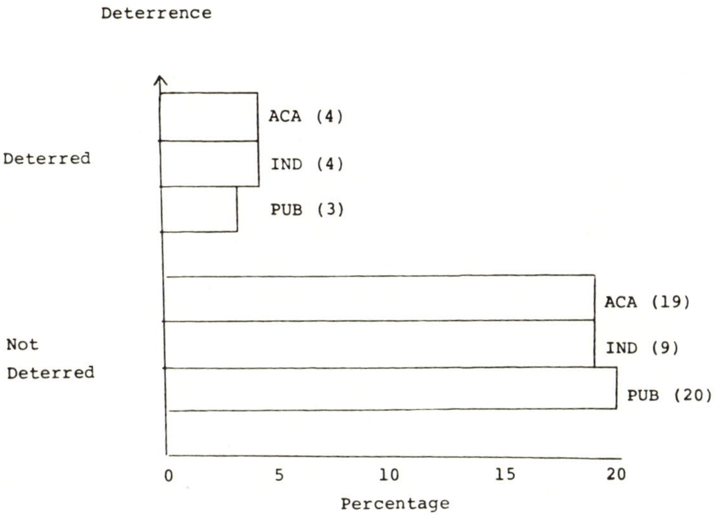
Deterrence
Deterred
ACA (4)
IND (4)
PUB (3)
Not
Deterred
ACA (19)
IND (9)
PUB (20)
0
5
10
15
20
Percentage

Figure 23. A Histogram of Sample Distribution by Fee Deterrence

Attitudes Toward Comprehensive Manual Literature Searches Services

Using Scheffé's procedure, analysis of variance was done to see whether there were significant differences in attitudes toward comprehensive manual literature searches among academic, public, and industrial library users.

Attitudes Toward Interlibrary Loans

As in other comparisons, analysis of variance was performed using Scheffé's test to compare attitudes toward interlibrary loans.

Attitudes Toward Specific Services by the Whole Sample

The second major hypothesis was that computerized bibliographical services are more acceptable as regards fees than comprehensive manual literature searches or interlibrary loans. Scheffé's S method was used to make all possible comparisons among means.[7] Scheffé has shown that the probability is $1 - \alpha$ that all possible contrasts will be captured by a set of intervals given by

148   The Information Dilemma

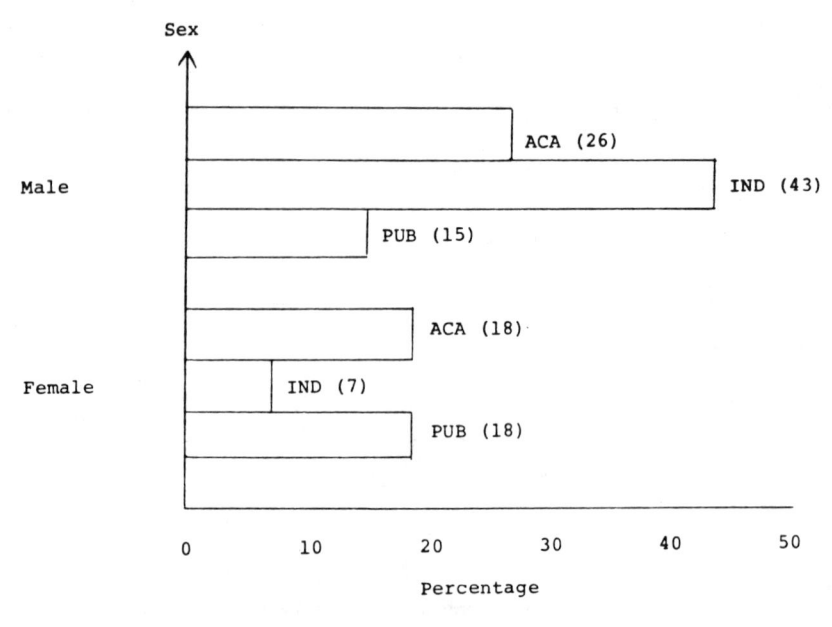

```
                    Sex
                     ↑
         ┌──────────────────────────────┐
         │              ACA (26)        │
         ├──────────────────────────────────────┐
Male     │                    IND (43)          │
         ├──────────────────┐
         │    PUB (15)      │
         └──────────────────┘
              ┌──────────────────┐
              │     ACA (18)     │
              ├──────┐
Female        │ IND (7)
              ├──────────────────┐
              │     PUB (18)     │
              └──────────────────┘

         0      10      20      30      40      50
                        Percentage
```

Figure 24. A Histogram of Sample Distribution by Sex

$$\hat{\psi} - S \leq \psi \leq \hat{\psi} + S$$

Where ψ and $\hat{\psi}$ refer to a population comparison and an estimate of the comparison, respectively. S is given by

$$S = \sqrt{(K-1) F\alpha; v_1, v_2} \sqrt{\text{MS error} \sum_{j=1}^{k} \frac{(CJ)^2}{nj}}$$

Where $F\alpha; v_1, v_2$ = tabled value of F for v_1 and v_2 degrees of freedom, K = number of treatment levels, Cj = coefficient of the contrast and nj = number of scores in the jth treatment level. In order for a comparison to be significant, it must be larger than the S as defined above.

Using this procedure, S was computed using values from the summary table thus:

Information Marketing Research   149

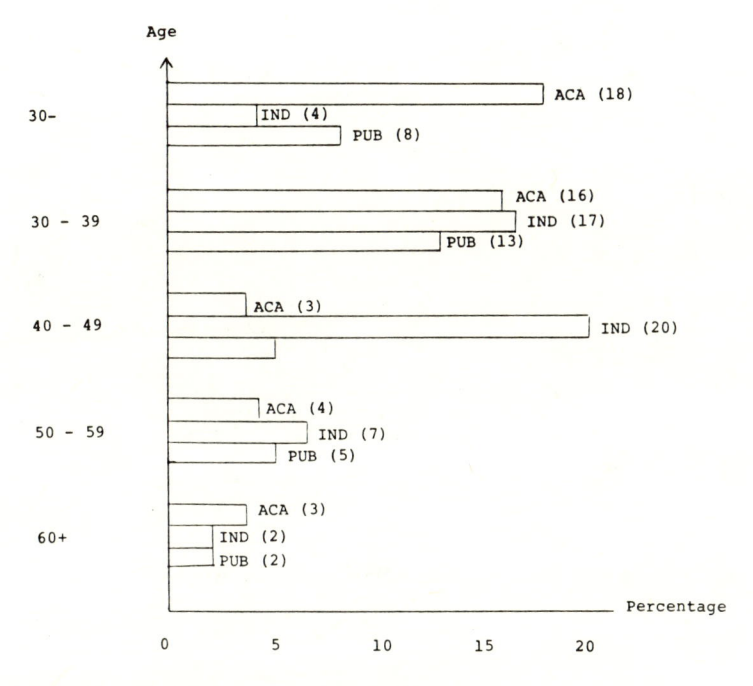

Figure 25. A Histogram of Sample Distribution by Age

$$S = \sqrt{(2)\ (3.04)} \sqrt{(.51947)\ (\frac{1+1}{127})} = .2230$$

A contrast between means greater than .2230 would indicate a statistically significant difference.

Comparison of Computerized Literature Search Services and Comprehensive Manual Searches

Given the null hypothesis:

150 The Information Dilemma

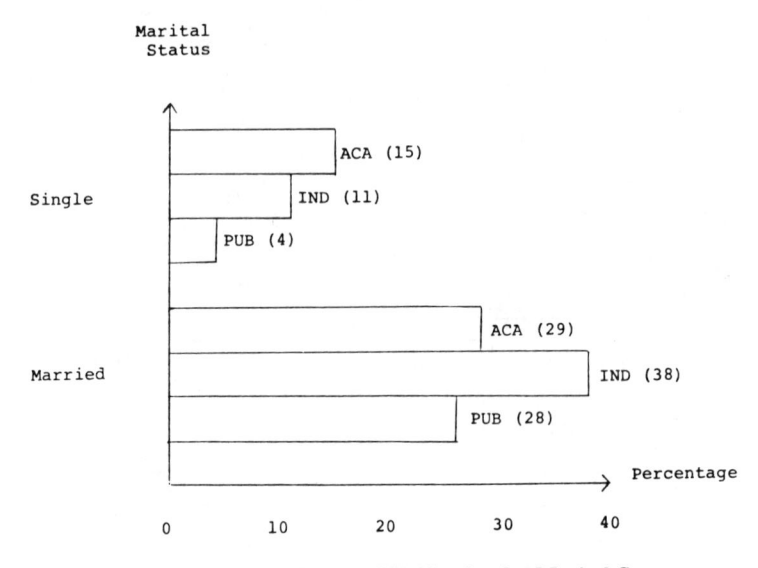

Figure 26. A Histogram of Sample Distribution by Marital Status

H_o $\psi = 0$
$\hat{\psi}$ = Contrast
$\hat{\psi} = B - C = 2.89764 - 2.39370$
$= 0.50394$

Where B = sample mean for computerized literature search services and C = sample mean for comprehensive manual literature searches.

In other words, there was a significant difference in attitudes towards computerized literature searches compared with comprehensive manual literature searches. Statistical analysis indicated a tendency for computerized literature searches to be less acceptable contrasted to comprehensive manual literature searches.

*Comparison of Computerized Literature Services
and Interlibrary Loans*

Given the null hypothesis:

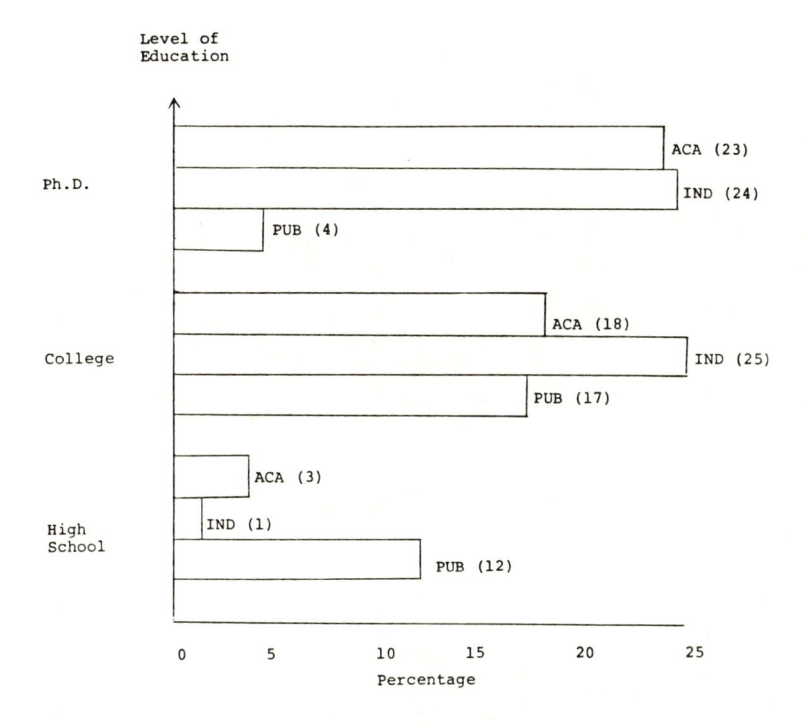

```
                    Level of
                    Education
                       ↑
                       |──────────────────────────────── ACA (23)
      Ph.D.           |──────────────────────────────────| IND (24)
                       |────── PUB (4)
                       |
                       |──────────────────────── ACA (18)
      College         |───────────────────────────────── IND (25)
                       |────────────────────── PUB (17)
                       |
                       |─── ACA (3)
      High            |── IND (1)
      School          |──────────── PUB (12)
                       |_____→
                       0    5    10   15   20   25
                              Percentage
```

Figure 27. A Histogram of Sample Distribution by Education

H_o: $\psi = 0$
$\hat{\psi} = $ Contrast
$\hat{\psi} = D - B = 3.22835 = 2.89764$
$\quad = 0.33071$

Where D = sample mean for interlibrary loans and B = sample mean for computerized literature search services. This also shows a statistically significant difference between computerized literature searches and interlibrary loans. According to the sample used, there was a tendency to accept fees for computerized literature search services more easily than for interlibrary loans.

Salary

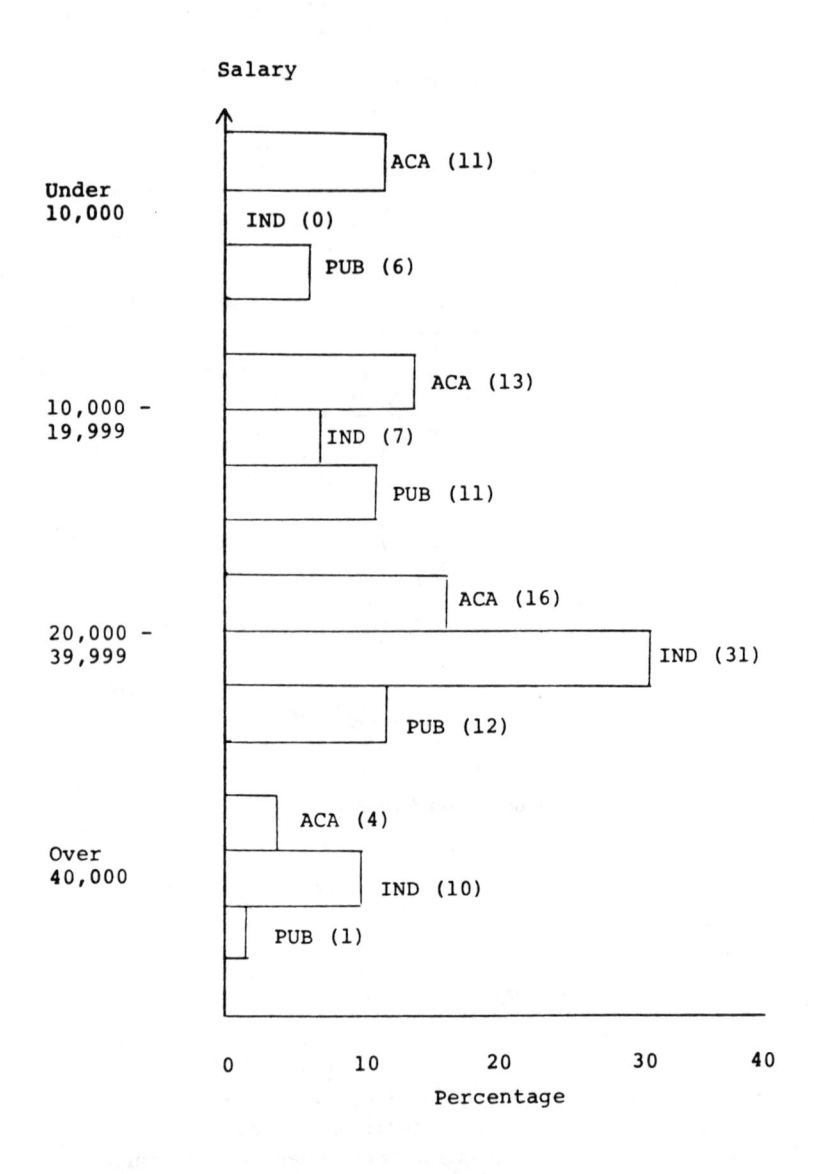

Salary Range	Category	Percentage
Under 10,000	ACA	(11)
	IND	(0)
	PUB	(6)
10,000 – 19,999	ACA	(13)
	IND	(7)
	PUB	(11)
20,000 – 39,999	ACA	(16)
	IND	(31)
	PUB	(12)
Over 40,000	ACA	(4)
	IND	(10)
	PUB	(1)

Percentage

Figure 28. A Histogram of Sample Distribution by Income

	Count	Mean	Standard Deviation	Standard Error
Academic	44	3.0591	0.7650	0.1153
Industrial	50	2.8280	0.6627	0.0937
Public	33	3.0485	0.9395	0.1635
Total	127	2.9654	0.7791	0.0691

Table 7. Mean Response to Section A—Deterrence

Source	DF	Sum of Squares	Mean Squares	F-Ratio	F-Prob
Between Groups	2	1.5580	0.7790	1.289	0.2792
Within Groups	124	74.9296	0.6043		
Total	126	76.4876			

At an alpha level of 0.05, there would be statistically significant differences if the F-probability were less than 0.05. In this case there was no significant differences among the groups. In other words, none of the three groups were different in their reaction to fees.

Table 8. Summary Table of the Analysis of Variance for Fees as a Deterrent

Source	DF	Sum of Squares	Mean Squares	F-Ratio	F-Prob
Between Groups	2	1.1192	0.5596	1.061	.3493
Within Groups	124	65.4024	0.5274		
Total	126	66.5216			

At an alpha level of 0.05 there would be significant differences if the F probability were less than 0.05. Thus in this case there were no significant differences in attitudes towards computerized literature search services. The groups means were all less than 3.0, which meant that they tended to accept fees for computerized literature searches.

Table 9. Summary Table of the Analysis of Variance for Computerized Literature Search Services

Source	DF	Sum of Squares	Mean Squares	F-Ratio	F-Prob
Between Groups	2	1.4714	0.7357	1.430	0.2431
Within Groups	124	63.7771	0.5143		
Total	126	65.2485			

With an alpha level of 0.05, there would be significant differences if the F probability were less than 0.05. In this case, there was no significant difference in attitudes towards comprehensive literature search services.

Table 10. Summary Table of the Analysis of Variance for Comprehensive Manual Literature Search Services

Source	DF	Sum of Squares	Mean Squares	F-Ratio	F-Prob
Between Groups	2	6.3188	3.1594	1.521	0.0340
Within Groups	124	122.7206	0.9090		
Total	126	119.0394			

Using an alpha level of 0.05, there would be significant differences if the F probability were less than 0.05. Thus, this indicated significant differences. Examining the possible comparisons revealed that there were no significant difference in attitudes between academic and industrial library users. Likewise, there were no significant differences between public library users and industrial library users. But there was a statistically significant difference between academic users and public library users. Looking at their grand means, public library users showed a tendency towards accepting fees for interlibrary loans, whereas academic library users showed the opposite tendency and therefore indicated rejection of fees for interlibrary loan services.

Table 11. Summary Table of the Analysis of Variance for Interlibrary Loans

Comparison of Comprehensive Manual Literature Services and Interlibrary Loans

Given the null hypothesis:

H_o: $\psi = 0$
$\hat{\psi}$ = Contrast
$\hat{\psi} = D - C = 3.22835 - 2.3970$
    $= 0.83465$

Where D = sample mean for interlibrary loans and C = sample mean for comprehensive manual literature searches.

A statistically significant difference existed in this pair of comparisons. In other words, given the sample used in the study, there was a tendency to accept fees more readily for comprehensive manual literature searches than for interlibrary loans.

Personal Interviews

Twelve interviews were conducted by the researcher to supplement the mail questionnaire. Most of the subjects for this exercise were selected at the same time as those for the mail questionnaire. For expediency, both face-to-face and telephone interview techniques were used.

Response patterns were comparable to those for the mail questionnaire. For instance, there were no significant differences in attitudes towards fees among the three categories of users: public library, academic library and industrial library user.

On the question of whether charging of fees is a deterrent to access to information by potential users, 67% responded that it was not, while 33% responded that it was. This was also comparable to the mail questionnaire responses depicted in Figure 23. Most respondents reasoned that a person's interests are usually satisfied without recourse to services that would require payment of a fee.

Opinions regarding payment for services were invariably accompanied by conditions like, "provided the fee was reasonable," and "provided the fee was not too high." For computer literature searches, 83% accepted paying in principle, whereas 17% rejected the idea. This is comparable to the questionnaire data.

As regards comprehensive manual literature searches, interviews revealed that very few people ever ask their libraries or information centers to do such a service for them. The tendency was to argue that if at all asked for, it should be part of a normal reference service. Consequently, 83% rejected paying for the service and 17% accepted it as justifying charges to the patron.

Finally, interlibrary loans were somewhat controversial. There were arguments on either side. In terms of statistics, 42% accepted payment for this service in principle and 58% rejected payment, arguing that the library should bear the cost.

INTERPRETATION OF THE PITTSBURGH STUDY FINDINGS

As an information marketing research project, the Pittsburgh study revealed new insights in the fees issues. In some cases, it confirmed earlier studies' findings. It can be replicated and the instrument which was developed and tested (Appendix A) may be utilized by managers of information centers and libraries for opinion surveys about clients.

The Research Methodology

One of the main objectives of this study was to develop a methodology to use in analyzing the fees issues as discussed in Chapter 5. Devising a research instrument for data collection was vital to this process. The first attempt was done at the pilot stage. Using item analysis, items which had a negative correlation were rephrased or replaced. The final instrument which appears as Appendix A was used for the main data collection exercise. On a second analysis a few more items still had negative correlations and these items were deleted from the final data computations.

High correlations were achieved when some of the items were dropped. According to these correlations, the items in subsets A-E measure the same or similar characteristics as reflected in user responses. Thus the instrument has a high internal validity.

Personal interviews, which were used to reinforce the results of the mail questionnaire, highlighted some aspects of the study. For instance, during the course of the interviews it was revealed that four basic factors influenced the individual's decision to accept or reject fees. In the first place, the amount was extremely important. It appeared as if there was a critical value at which one would accept charges and above which one would not. Secondly, urgency of information was another factor. Depending on the relative urgency, the individual might accept payment for information if it was needed by a specific time. Thirdly, several respondents indicated willingness to pay if the information was vital to their existence, especially when it is job related. Finally, acceptance was greatly affected by lack of alternative sources for the needed information. It is important to note that the fundamental reasons for accepting fees or rejecting them were essentially pragmatic rather than philosophical. In the opinion of the researcher, the methodology was adequate for the analysis of the main issues addressed by the study.

Major Hypotheses Testing

The study had significant findings, in spite of the sampling problems. The major hypotheses were analyzed as follows:

First Hypothesis

The first hypothesis, that fees are a deterrent to library use, was not supported by the findings of the study. Response patterns indicated that fees were not a deterrent to access to information.

Second Hypothesis

The second hypothesis, that industrial library users accept fees more readily than academic or public library users, was also rejected. It was based on the assumption that industrial based users have higher salaries than average and thus more disposable income. In addition, they would have more company funds to spend on information. On the contrary, statistical tests indicated no significant difference of opinion compared to the other two categories. But it was revealed that public library users' attitudes towards interlibrary loans differed from those of academic library users. Whereas academic users showed a tendency to reject fees for interlibrary loans, public library users showed a tendency to accept fees for such services.

Third Hypothesis

The third hypothesis was that fees for computerized literature search services are more acceptable compared with comprehensive manual searches or interlibrary loans. This hypothesis was partially upheld. Judged by the three services addressed by this study, acceptance patterns differed on the three pairs. Comparing computerized literature searches and comprehensive manual searches revealed a statistically significant difference. It was shown that there was a tendency for fees for computerized literature searches to be less acceptable than comprehensive manual literature searches. However, both services had low means, indicating that both were in the realm of acceptance. As mentioned earlier, personal interviews revealed that a small number of people expected the library to carry out comprehensive manual literature searches for them. This might thus reveal the feeling that since few people ever ask for such services, they should pay for them.

Comparing computerized literature searches and interlibrary loans revealed statistically significant difference in attitudes. In our sample, there was a tendency to accept fees for computer searches more readily than for interlibrary loans. Checking the means showed a clear rejection for interlibrary loans. Interview results were comparable to mail questionnaire findings. One of the main arguments for rejecting fees for interlibrary loans was that the parent library should have adequate materials for its patrons. Where materials are insufficient, interlibrary loans should be part of the internal working of the library with no extra charge to the patron.

The pairing exercise for interlibrary loans and comprehensive manual literature searches revealed that our sample accepted fees for comprehensive manual literature searches more readily than for interlibrary loans. As partly explained before, interlibrary loans were regarded as an integral part of a library or information center's operations. Conversely, comprehensive manual literature searches were deemed rare services demanded by only a few members of the clientele.

Response Patterns and Categories of Users

Some of the response patterns of the three categories of users were similar to earlier studies done elsewhere. As the research design for this study had a unique orientation, comparisons can only be made on certain common parameters.

Academic Information Users

Academic library users had a positive disposition towards fees, which is comparable to earlier studies, for example, Hitchingham's study,[8] Cogswell,[9] and Kobelski and Trumbore.[10] However, this must be qualified, for as stated earlier, price, value, urgency, and alternative sources are major factors in making the final decision. In addition this study indicated that academics would be resentful if charges were to be instituted for interlibrary loans.

Industrial Information Users

As a sub-group industrial information users had very similar responses to academics. Although as company employees they had ample funds for information, they also felt that for interlibrary loans, the company's information center should bear the cost and not the individual department they may be working in.

Public Library Users

As a subgroup public library users did not show an adverse disposition to being charged for fees. Interviews brought out interesting discussions about fees. For example, the argument that charging fees was a double charge in terms of the tax-dollar and then extra charge for a service, was dismissed. Two counter arguments were advanced. First, several people argued that they do pay for museums and parks as well as highways which are publicly supported utilities. Second, it was argued that these are additional services which are rarely asked for by the ordinary public library user. This positive disposition towards fees was similar to the findings of the DIALIB study.

NOTES

1. David A. Aaker and George S. Day, *Marketing Research: Private and Public Sector Decisions* (New York: John Wiley & Sons, 1980), pp. 1-43.

2. William J. Stanton, *Fundamentals of Marketing*, 6th ed. (New York: McGraw-Hill, 1981), p. 43.

3. *Home Terminal Services, Consumer Survey Results* (Atlanta, Ga.: Payment Systems, Inc., 1981).

4. Michael D. Cooper and Nancy A. Dewath, "The Effect of User Fees on the Cost of On-Line Searching in Libraries," *Journal of Library Automation* 9 (September 1976):195-209.

5. Alan R. Benefield, *et al.*, "User Receptivity to Fee for Service Computer-Based Reference in a University Community," *ASIS Proceedings* 12 (1975):158-59.

6. Fred N. Kerlinger, *Foundations of Behavioral Research* (New York: Holt, Rinehart and Winston, 1973), pp. 129-30.

7. Roger E. Kirk, *Experimental Design: Procedures for Behavioral Sciences* (Belmont, Calif.: Brooks/Cole Publishing Co., 1968), pp. 90-91.

8. Eileen E. Hitchingham, "Use of Commercially Vended Online Data Bases by Academic Libraries," *ASIS Proceedings* 12 (1975):158-59.

9. James A. Cogswell, "On-line Search Services: Implications for Libraries and Library Users," *College and Research Libraries* 39 (July 1978):276.

10. Pamela Kobelski and Jean Trumbore, "Student Use of Online Bibliographical Services," *Journal of Academic Librarianship* 4 (1978):14-18.

9
Conclusion

We have in *The Information Dilemma* attempted to present a macro collective overview highlighting some of the dominant issues of the Information Age. Most of these issues have been catapulted into society by electronic devices particularly the digital computer. Issues have been analyzed as they relate to systems designers, information resources or data processing managers, corporation executives, educators, government officials, managers of information centers and libraries, database vendors, information brokers and information users.

The end result is a telescopic view focussing on computer-based information handling problems. The book gradually builds up from the general concepts in the first two chapters to more pragmatic problems of pricing information products, management of information resources, the fees controversy, legal issues in accessing large information data banks, and information marketing research.

What started as small scale devices to help human effort in harnessing the intractable information explosion resulted in multifaceted information networks. The environment of information processing has attained very volatile and dynamic tenets which dazzle the user and sometimes the designer. As stressed in the text, one of the fundamental issues facing information policy planners is accessibility to vital information during the Information Age, when acquisition of information is invaluable to existence. How about international barriers? Structures exist at both bilateral and multi-lateral levels to negotiate relatively free flow of information. While the United Nations has been criticized for its slow pace in reacting to international conflicts, it has served as a forum for airing disputes. Some of its agencies like UNESCO (United Nations Educational, Scientific and Cultural Organization) and GATT (General Agreement on Tariffs and Trade) will attain special roles in the so called "transborder data flow."

Constant technological change will continue to thrust puzzles into the information arena. Accelerated obsolescence may be deterred by what equipment manufacturers term upward compatibility, whereby old machines may be slightly modified to operate like later inventions. In practical terms, compatibility does not appear to have succeeded as manufacturers predict.

Current trends in information technology indicate that fifth generation computers of the 1980s will be smaller, faster and relatively easy to use. In addition, users are getting more power per dollar of investment. While intersystem connection may remain a problem for some time, the performance of computer-based information networks has improved remarkably. Microwave and satellite data communications have facilitated long distance interconnections which had hitherto been impossible.

With the increased and increasing proliferation of information processing devices in the factory, the office and the home, it is imperative for institutions to automate most of their operations. Office automation is now beyond the fad stage into practical realities, whereby teleconferencing—conducting discussions simultaneously at long distances—is in practice. The integration of word processing, electronic mail, computer graphics, facsimile transmission and micro computers has revolutionized business, educational and governmental functions. To be successful in the Information Age, institutions, regardless of size, must keep abreast of these developments. There is Catch 22, however, conceptualized in the bandwagon effect. The path to effective automation is strewn with skeletons of failed systems and disappointed information users. Limited information marketing research as discussed in Chapter 8 is sometimes needed before committing institutional funds to large scale operations. In other words, we should not automate for automation's sake, for some functions are more cost effective when done manually.

As explored in this book, the information scene in the United States is a microcosm of the Information Age. This is partly because of the large scale capital investment in information technology. It is one thing to have ingenious concepts, it is quite another to develop them into tangible marketable products. While a sizable amount of "seed" money was ploughed into technology by the U.S. under sponsored research, private investors have responded very favorably to high technology stock and bond sales. Relatively young corporations like Apple Computers, Wang Laboratories, Amdahl and Magnuson have flourished on both ingenuity and high private capital financing.

The hardware industry which is a vital component of information technology is experiencing continuous miniaturization of components. In addition the user has a wide array of different brands, which makes selection a problem. As smaller computers become more powerful and relatively less costly, there is a general tendency to get away from mainframes and a preference for microcomputers. This trend makes even those people who never dreamed of owning a computer capable of buying personal computers. In addition, small organizations including information centers and libraries can now effectively automate several of their functions. As for growth rates, smaller computers are growing faster than large mainframes.

With an increased multiplicity of user interests, software (programs which run computers) is commanding a big chunk of the information industry. It is now possible to have a variety of off-the-shelf packages which perform several of the daily institutional routines like inventory control, accounting and statistical analysis.

Perhaps the most pervasive feature of the Information Age is the growth of very large data banks. Whether private or government owned, data banks have the convenience of remote access at locations of choice via data communication lines. But with convenience has come the tying up of vital information which used to be available in printed form. As has been amply demonstrated, measures must be taken to ensure that researchers who genuinely cannot pay, have access to publicly available data banks.

Ease of use is increasing the tempo of information consumption. The market is expanding at an exponential rate with the result that well designed and marketed products are guaranteed immediate public acceptance.

How about user access to information services and products? That is where human factors come in. While we perfect methods of information processing and data communications, we should simultaneously emphasize user access. Industrialized countries have built enormous societal and institutional computer-based data banks. As we progress deeper into the Information Age, these data banks continue to gobble most of the information which used to be available in "hard printed copy" forms. Several issues arise. First, how easy to use are these data banks? Information professionals may claim that the information systems they design are "user friendly." With regard to personal computer software packages one user referred to them as torture chambers,[1] with reference to ease of use! The systems designed in the 1970s and early 1980s were not user friendly even to sophisticated users. This curtailed optimum use of available data banks. Second, information tied up in the data banks may not be readily available to users of public information centers or libraries because of the cost. At the present moment, when a lot of information is still available in printed form, charging fees is not a major deterrent to bona fide information seekers. This may not be true in the later part of the 1980s decade. Third, personal, private and sensitive information contained in data banks must be guarded against unauthorized access.

When information becomes highly commercialized as a commodity, it is inevitable to use acceptable pricing methods to arrive at equitable prices. If the objective of pricing is cost recovery, one must decide what cost is being recovered. One may have to determine whether fixed costs, variable costs or total costs are being recovered. In addition, one must decide on the method of determining price—demand based pricing, competition based pricing or cost based pricing.

The management of information resources is another prime issue of the Information Age. Productivity depends on how well information technologies are coordinated and managed within an organization. To achieve high productivity different types of information technologies—data processing, data communications, library technology, computer based reprography and others—must be re-organized to form a unified organizational information function. This applies to both public and private institutions. Data processing departments as organized in the 1970s can no longer accommodate the new technologies which are essentially at equal levels of service provision. Consequently, an information coordination unit must be instituted to ensure that components of the institutional network do not duplicate services or pursue conflicting interests.

Finally, introduction of new services and products raises questions of acceptability by clients. This in turn may depend on what similar products or services are available on the market. Competing organizations and what marketing strategies they use may yet be another consideration. A closer look at these problems reveals that they are basically marketing research issues. Information marketing research which must be a significant tenet of the Information Age is the data collection and analysis element of information product and service development. It is client oriented and should help the decision maker in deciding whether a new product or service should either be introduced or continued.

The total picture in the information arena is larger than the sum of the component parts. Let the systems designers see beyond bits and bytes and design systems which are more than user friendly—and perhaps be "seductive."[2] Let the information professionals see beyond their own convenience to the convenience of the users. Let data processing managers look beyond the central computing unit as the hub of all information processing, for there are other challengers. As we plunge into the deep end of the Information Age, shocks are not over yet, but they will be less painful if we see them in perspective.

NOTES

1. Peter Nulty, "Apple's Bid to Stay in the Big Time," *Fortune* (February 7, 1983):36-41.

2. *Ibid.*, p. 38.

Appendix A

The Information Use Questionnaire

Please read each statement carefully and respond to the request as appropriate. There is no right or wrong answer. Kindly circle the number for each statement and do not leave any statement unmarked. Categories are as follows:

Strongly Agree (1)	Agree (2)	Undecided (3)	Disagree (4)	Strongly Disagree (5)

A. Some libraries charge fees for some of the services they provide. Please give your opinion on questions 1-6.

1. Potential users are denied access to information when fees are charged in libraries.   1 2 3 4 5

2. Anybody needing information will get it whether or not a library charges fees.   1 2 3 4 5

3. Fees are a major deterrent to library use.   1 2 3 4 5

4. Students are denied access to information by charging fees in libraries.   1 2 3 4 5

5. Information may be so urgent that user   1 2 3 4 5
   fees are not significant.

6. Due to charges, researchers with no   1 2 3 4 5
   grants are denied access to vital
   information.

B. Computers are sometimes used to get information for users
   and the library pays $5 to maybe $100 or more. Please
   respond to questions 7-12.

7. Library budgets should accommodate com-   1 2 3 4 5
   puter literature searches for users.

8. In a public library computer literature   1 2 3 4 5
   searches are a waste of money to the
   general public.

9. Individuals requesting computerized   1 2 3 4 5
   literature searches in a library should
   be charged.

10. Computerized literature searches should   1 2 3 4 5
    be part of the normal library services.

11. Computer printouts give a large amount   1 2 3 4 5
    of useless information and are not
    worth the cost.

12. Extra costs should be charged to the   1 2 3 4 5
    requesting patron rather than
    eliminating computer services.

C. Library users sometimes request that librarians perform
   comprehensive literature searches. This may take per-

Appendix A   169

haps 1-8 hours or even days of the librarian's time, without using computer aids. Please respond to questions 13-18.

13. Library users requesting comprehensive manual literature searches should be charged.   1 2 3 4 5

14. Users should do their own comprehensive manual literature searches.   1 2 3 4 5

15. Comprehensive manual literature searches are part of a normal library service and should be free.   1 2 3 4 5

16. Users prefer to do their own comprehensive manual literature searches rather than pay for them.   1 2 3 4 5

17. Comprehensive manual literature searches are a special favor to individual patrons, and should be charged.   1 2 3 4 5

18. Comprehensive manual literature searches are difficult to price, thus should not be charged for.   1 2 3 4 5

D. Sometimes a library borrows from other libraries materials on behalf of its users. It may be charged $8 or more per item borrowed. Please respond to questions 19-24.

19. Interlibrary loan is not a normal service and should be charged to individuals.   1 2 3 4 5

20. Interlibrary loans are vital to reader   1 2 3 4 5
    interests and should be free.
21. Interlibrary loans are custom tailored   1 2 3 4 5
    and should be charged to library users.
22. The library's general budget should   1 2 3 4 5
    accommodate interlibrary loans.
23. If all interlibrary loans were free,   1 2 3 4 5
    readers would abuse the privilege.
24. Only a small portion of readers   1 2 3 4 5
    request materials from other libraries
    and should pay the extra cost.
E. It is sometimes necessary for the user to assess the
    relevance of materials received from the library.
    Please respond to questions 25-32.
25. Computerized literature searches make   1 2 3 4 5
    no substantial contribution to the
    researchers effectiveness.
26. Speed is important and quick computer   1 2 3 4 5
    searches are invaluable to a library
    user.
27. Computer printouts are usually irrele-   1 2 3 4 5
    vant to the initial problem.
28. Librarians are not competent to do   1 2 3 4 5
    searches for technical experts.
29. Work colleagues provide more job-related   1 2 3 4 5
    information than the library.

30. Researchers prefer to do their own   1 2 3 4 5
    literature search manually.
31. Computer literature searches are not   1 2 3 4 5
    worth the charges.
32. Delegation of literature search to a   1 2 3 4 5
    librarian saves the user's time.
 F. Please check only one item appropriate to you for each question.
33. Area of speciality:
    Science ( ), Social Science ( ), Humanities ( ), Not Applicable ( ).
34. Status:
    Student ( ), Faculty ( ), Research Scientist ( ), Administrator ( ), Not Applicable ( ).
35. Have you ever worked on a project funded by the government or other agency?
    Yes ( ), No ( )
36. Have you ever used a computerized literature search service?
    Yes ( ), No ( )
37. If the answer to question 36 is no, did fees influence your decision?
    Yes ( ), No ( )
38. Male ( ), Female ( )
39. Age: Under 30 ( ), 30-39 ( ), 40-49 ( ), 50-59 ( ), 60 or over ( ).

40. Single ( ), Married ( )
41. Education:

    Ph.D. or equivalent ( ), College ( ), High School and below ( ).
42. Your annual salary:

    Under $10,000 ( )

    $10,000-19,999 ( )

    $20,000-39,999 ( )

    $40,000 or over ( )

Appendix B
Glossary of Terms

Analog signal A signal which is formed by a continuous range of amplitudes or frequencies; for instance, a continuously varying current or the human voice.

ARPANET A large packet-switched communications network developed by the Department of Defense in 1969. It continues to serve as a model for this type of network.

Artificial intelligence The concept that machines can be improved to assume some capabilities normally thought to be like human intelligence such as learning, adapting, self-correction, etc.

Batch processing A technique by which similar data to be processed are accumulated into groups or batches in advance and processed during one computer run.

Bit (binary digit) May be a 0 or a 1, the digits used in the binary numbering system.

BRS Bibliographic Retrieval Services.

Byte A sequence of adjacent bits which are treated as a unit. Ordinarily, a character is represented by one or two bytes.

CAD/CAM Programs that make up computer-aided design and computer-aided manufacturing systems.

CAI Computer Assisted Instruction. A concept which applies computers and specialized input/output display devices directly to individualized student instruction.

CAN-OLE Canadian On-line Enquiry.

CATV Cable or community TV: A system with two-way capacity to conduct signals to the lead end as well as away from it, providing entertainment and education programs to customers on a coaxial cable system for a fee.

Central processing unit (CPU) Part of a computing system which contains circuits to execute instructions in order to intelligently accomplish a desired objective.

CHEMLINE A database produced by the U.S. National Library of Medicine. It is an on-line chemical dictionary file containing various nomenclature.

Chip A tiny piece of silicon on which an integrated circuit is built, the circuits being mass-produced on circular sheets of silicon called wafers that are then cut into dozens of individual chips, often square or rectangular.

COM Computer output on microfilm.

Compunications A term used to denote integrated data processing and transfer systems using computers and data communications or telecommunications.

COMSAT Communications Satellite Corporation. Represented by more than 85 members of the INTELSAT Organization to provide technical and operational services for the global satellite communications system under a management contract with INTELSAT, headquartered in Washington, D.C.

Connect time Time period during which a user is accessing a computer system.

CRT Cathode ray tube. A television like display device attached to a computer or used as a remote terminal.

Cybernetics A field of science relating the operation of automatic equipment to functions of the human nervous system.

Data bank A collection of data that relate to a given set of subjects.

Database A collection of files which are interrelated to reduce redundancy, provide for data independence, security, integrity and reliability.

Data communications Electronic transmission of encoded data from one location to another.

DBMS Database management systems.

DIALOG A dial up information retrieval service offered by Lockheed Information Retrieval System.

Digital signal A signal which is formed by discrete electrical pulses using a two state or binary system.

Direct access Any method of accessing data in which the time required for such access is independent of the storage location. It is also known as *random access method*.

Disk drive A direct access device used to read from and record data on a magnetic disk.

DOS (disk operating system) A versatile operating system for IBM 360 computer systems having disk capability.

Dumb terminal A terminal which can perform input or output to a computer system, but has no data processing capabilities.

EDP Electronic data processing.

Ergonomics The study of human capability and psychology in relation to the working environment and the equipment operated by the worker.

EURONET A computer-based European network. It was established by the European Economic Community to access scientific and other data banks running on host computers connected to the network in different countries.

Facsimile A method of transmitting paper documents, pictures, etc. by communications channels (e.g. telephone). The document is scanned at the transmitter and reconstructed at the receiver.

Failsafe A procedure which allows the computer to store certain data from its own memory when it detects that it is failing e.g. through loss of power. It facilitates easy recovery of data in case of accidental malfunction.

Fiber optics Cables composed of glass fibers which carry data through pulses of a laser beam.

Flip-flop A circuit capable of assuming either of two stable states.

Floppy disk Flexible disk of magnetic coated mylar. It provides low cost storage and is used in mini computer and micro computer systems.

FOIA Freedom of Information Act.

Gigabyte One billion bytes.

Hardware Computer and data processing equipment, the electronic and mechanical devices, the equipment itself as contrasted with software and firmware.

Informatics Studies related to information systems design analysis and evaluation.

Information An aggregation of data with assignable meaning.

Input/Output Refers to the insertion of data or instructions into a computer or transfer of processed data from the computer to the user. Examples of input/output media are: cathode ray tubes, punched cards, disks and printers.

Integrated circuit The entire circuit, including active and passive components built on a chip. Integrated circuits result in small size, high reliability, low cost and high speed.

Intelligent terminal A terminal with internal logic circuitry, which allows some functions to be done at the terminal, such as syntax error editing.

Interactive computer graphics The use of computer terminals for drawing lines and images.

K When referring to storage capacity of computer systems or components, 2^{10}, in decimal notation 1024.

Large Scale Integration (LSI) Fabrication of circuits with a large number of transistors on a single chip.

LEXIS Data bank on law literature developed by Mead Corporation.

Light pen A stylus used with CRT display devices to edit information on the CRT screen.

Magnetic bubble memory Very high capacity chips which use small cylindrical magnetic domains ("bubbles") which move over the surface of a magnetic film. The presence of a bubble corresponds to a "1" bit and the absence of a bubble to a "0" bit.

Magnetic core memory Main memories made of iron cores, which can be magnetized in either of two directions. Such memories have been gradually replaced by memories using semiconductors.

Magnetic disk A storage device consisting of a magnetized recording surface on a metal disk.

Magnetic tape A plastic tape coated with magnetic material upon which data may be recorded.

Mainframe The CPU (Central Processing Unit) of a computer (doesn't include any of the other devices such as input/output, etc.). The term has been extended to mean the large types of computer systems.

Main memory The internal storage in a computer, used to store data being processed.

MEDLARS Medical literature analysis and retrieval system, developed by the U.S. National Library of Medicine.

MEDLINE MEDLARS on line—a computer based data bank developed by the U.S. National Library of Medicine. It contains literature on medical sciences and biological sciences.

Megabyte One million bytes.

Microcomputer A general term referring to a complete tiny computer system, consisting of hardware and software whose main processing blocks are made of semiconductor integrated circuits and that is similar in function and structure to a minicomputer but is at least several orders cheaper due to mass production; components are: ALU (arithmetic-logic unit), memory, peripheral circuits, such as input-output, clock, control devices.

Microfiche The most popular COM or Computer Output Microfilm format, a fiche is approximately 4" × 6" and can include an eye-readable title row, often up to 269 dataframes at the 48X reduction ratio, and an index frame.

Microprocessor A central processing unit constructed on a single chip. Microprocessors are used in micro computers and intelligent terminals.

Microsecond One millionth of a second.

MOS Metal oxide semiconductor.

MTBF Mean time between failures.

MTTR Mean time to repair. The time it takes to get the system back to normal working condition after a failure.

Multiprocessing The use of two or more computer processing units in the same system at the same time.

Multiprogramming A system with the ability to effectively process programs concurrently.

Nanosecond One billionth of a second.

Network A set of locations (nodes) connected by communications channels.

NLM National Library of Medicine.

OCLC On-line computer library center.

OCR (Optical Character Recognition) Using photosensitive (optical) devices to sense (read) characters.

Offline A term used to describe equipment, devices, or persons not in direct communication with the central processing unit of a computer system. Equipment which is not connected to the computer system contrast with on-line.

On-line An on-line system is one in which the input data enter the computer directly from their point of origin and/or output data are transmitted directly to where they are used. The intermediate stages such as punching data, writing tape, loading disks, or offline printing are avoided.

Operating system Programs which manage the hardware resources and the data for a computer system.

Operations research The application of objective and quantitative criteria to decision making previously undertaken by empirical methods.

ORBIT A dial up information retrieval service offered by Systems Development Corporation.

Paging In virtual storage systems, the technique of making memory appear larger than it is by transferring blocks (pages) of data or programs into that memory from external storage when they are needed.

Picosecond One trillionth of a second. Sometimes spelled "pecosecond."

POP Print on paper.

Protocol A set of conventions between communicating processes on the format and content of messages as well as the speed to be exchanged. In sophisticated networks higher level protocols may use lower protocols in a layered fashion.

Real time Time during which a physical process actually takes place. A real time data processing system performs computations rapidly enough for the results to influence the event.

Remote terminal An input/output device that is located at a remote distance from a computer system. It is used to input programs and data to a computer and to accept computed data from a computer.

Response time The amount of time that elapses between the presentation of a transaction to a system and the completion of processing that transaction.

RLIN Research Libraries Information Network.
Robot A completely self-controlled electronic, electric, or mechanical device. Most Information Age robots will be computer controlled.
Robotics Study, analysis, design and operation of robots.
SCP System control program.
SDC Systems Development Corporation.
Semiotics The study of relationships between signs or symbols and what they signify or denote.
Sequential Refers to occurrence of events in time sequence with little or no overlap of events.
Software All the programming systems and programs used to support a computer. The computer or equipment itself is called *hardware*.
Solid state The electronic components which convey or control electrons within solid materials—for example, transistors, germanium diodes and magnetic cores.
Tape drive A sequential access device used to read from and record data on a magnetic tape.
Telecommunication To transmit or receive signals, sounds or intelligence of any nature by wire, light beam or any other means.
Teleconferencing A conference between people who are linked by a telecommunications system. The link in increasing order of complication and cost, can be telephone, group audio or video.
Telematic Anglicized term from French term "telematique." It means information processing using computers and telecommunications.
TELENET A U.S. based commercial international data communications network.
Teleprocessing The combination of computers and communications networks in an information processing system.
Teletype A device with a keyboard and printing capabilities, used to enter information into a computer and to accept output. It looks like a typewriter.
Time-sharing A technique by which available computer time is shared among several users. This is done by timewise interleaving of processor requests by different users. It occurs so fast that users are not aware of it.
TOS (Tape Operating System) An operating system of System 360 computers used in magnetic tape, no random access system.
Transistor A device made by attaching three or more wires to a small wafer of semiconductor material (a single crystal that has been specially treated so that its properties are different at the point where each wire is attached). The three wires are usually called the emitter, base, and collector. They perform functions somewhat similar to those of the cathode, grid, and plate of a vacuum tube, respectively.
UPC Universal Product code. The symbols in the form of vertical bars of varying widths reflect light emitted by an optical scanner, the code numbers going to computers for transmission to other sources and to control printing devices to provide customer receipts after the computer responds with the identification of the product and the price.
Utility programs Programs often supplied by the hardware manufacturer, for executing standard operations such as sorting, merging, reformationing data, renaming files and comparing files.

Very large scale integration (VLSI). Fabrication of circuits with a very large number of transistors on a single chip.

Videodisk A disk on which optical images may be stored. Videodisks are often written and read using laser beams.

Wand A device for reading labels on retail goods in a point-of-scale automation system.

WLN Washington Library Network.

Word A set of characters which occupies one storage location and is treated by the control unit as a quantity. Word lengths may be fixed or variable depending on the particular computer.

WP (Word Processing) Interactive information-retrieval systems, management information systems, text editing, translation and typesetting systems controlled by.

Selected Bibliography

Annual Mini-Micro Survey. *Datamation* 27 (November 1981): 110-36.

Archibold, Pamela. "The Foremost U.S. Companies in the Data Processing Industry." *Datamation* 128 (June 1982): 114-226.

Artandi, Susan. "Computers and the Postindustrial Society: Symbiosis or Information Tyranny?" *Journal of the American Society for Information Science* 33 (September, 1982):303-7.

———"Man, Information and Society: New Patterns of Interaction." *Journal of the American Society for Information Science* 30 (January 1979):16-19.

Ashman, Richard D. "Advances in COM Provide Greater Productivity and Flexibility." *Information and Records Management* 15 (September 1981):67-73.

Avedon, Don. "The Automated Office." *Information and Records Management* 15 (April 1981):26-30.

Badler, Mitchell. "COM: A Records Medium for the '80s." *Information and Records Management* 16 (January 1982):23, 24, and 26.

Bell, Daniel. *The Coming of the Post-Industrial Society.* New York: Basic Books, Inc., 1973.

Berkeley, Alfred R. "Millionaire Machine?" *Datamation* 27 (August 1981):20-36.

Birks, Christine I. *Information Services in the Market Place. Research and Development Reports*, no. 5430. London: The British Library, July 1978.

Blair, John C. "Micros, Minis and Mainframes...A Newcomer's Guide to the World of Computers—Especially Micros." *Online* 6 (January 1982):14-26.

Selected Bibliography

Block, Victor. "Transborder Data Flow: Barriers to Free Flow of Information." *Infosystems* 28 (September 1981): 108-114.

Bolton, Theodore W. "A Lesson in Interactive Television Programming: The Home Book Club on QUBE." *Journal of Library Automation* 14 (June 1981):103-110.

Bourne, Charles P. "On-line Systems: History, Technology, and Economics." *Journal of the American Society for Information Science* 31 (May 1980):155-160.

Brenner, Everett H. "Euronet and Its Effects on the U.S. Information Market." *Journal of the American Society for Information Science* 30 (January 1979):5-8.

Bush, Vennevar. "As We May Think." *Atlantic Monthly* 176 (July 1945):101-108.

Buss, Martin D. J. "Managing International Information Systems." *Harvard Business Review* 60 (Sept.-Oct. 1982):153-162.

Clintone, Marshall, and Grenville, Sally. "Using European Systems from a North American Library." *Online* 4 (April 1980):22-27.

Connell, John J. "The Fallacy of Information Resource Management." *Infosystems* 28 (May 1981):78-84.

Corasick, M. J., and Brockway, B. G. "Protection of Computer-Based Information." *Albany Law Review* 40 (1975): 113-153.

Cravis, Howard. "Local Networks for the 1980s." *Datamation* 27 (March 1981):98-104.

Cundiff, Edward, et al. *Fundamentals of Modern Marketing.* Englewood Cliffs, N. J.: Prentice-Hall, 1976.

Davis, William and McCormack, Alison. *The Information Age.* Reading, Mass.: Addison-Wesley, 1979.

Debons, Anthony. *The Information Professional: Survey of an Emergent Field.* New York: Marcel Dekker, 1981.

DeGennaro, Richard. "Library Automation: Changing Patterns and New Directions." *Library Journal* 101 (January 1976):175-183.

―――"Research Libraries Enter the Information Age." *Library Journal* 104 (November 15, 1979): 2405-2410.

Dertouzos, Michael L., and Moses, Joel, eds. *The Computer Age: A Twenty-Year View.* Cambridge Mass.: MIT Press, 1979.

Disman, Murray. "Software Trends in Western Europe." *Datamation* 27 (August 1981):40-53.

Dolotta, T.A. *Data Processing in 1980-1985.* New York: John Wiley, 1976.

Edwards, Morris. "Battle of the Satellites." *Infosystems* 28 (May 1981):54-60.

―――"Computer-Based PBX: Heart and Brain of Office Automation." *Infosystems* 29 (January 1982): 72, 74, 76, & 78.

Selected Bibliography 181

———"Data Communications Directions." *Infosystems* 29 (January 1982):34-38.

———"Datacomm Directions: Modern and Multiplexer Update: Compact and Cheaper." *Infosystems* 28 (November 1981): 50-58.

———"Electronic Mail: Something for Everyone." *Infosystems* 28 (March 1981):54-62.

Epstein, Hank. "The Technology of Library and Information Networks." *Journal of the American Society for Information Science* 31 (November 1980):425-437.

Farmer, Dale F. "IBM Compatible Giants." *Datamation* 27 (December 1981):92-104.

Froehlich, Leopold. "Robots to the Rescue." *Datamation* 27 (January 1981):84-96.

Garvin, Andrew D. *How to Win with Information or Lose Without It*. Washington, D.C.: Bermont Books, 1980.

Grosch, Audrey N. "Library Automation." *Annual Review of Information Science and Technology* 11 (1976):225-266.

Gunn, Thomas G. *Computer Applications in Manufacturing*. New York: Industrial Press, Inc., 1981.

Halevi, Gideon. *The Role of Computers in Manufacturing Processes*. New York: Wiley, 1980.

Holoien, Martin O. *Computers and Their Societal Impact*. New York: Wiley, 1977.

Horton, Forest Woody, Jr. "The Paperwork Reduction Act of 1980—Reality at Last." *Information and Records Management* 15 (April 1981):10-12.

Huskey, Harry D. "Computer Technology." *Annual Review of Information Science and Technology* 5 (1970):73-85.

The Information Community: An Alliance for Progress. Proceedings of the 44th Annual Conference of the American Society for Information Science. Washington, D.C.: American Society for Information Science, 1981.

Kemeney, John G. *Man and the Computer*. New York: Scribner's, 1972.

Kent, Allen, and Galvin, Thomas J. *Library Resource Sharing*. New York: Marcel Dekker, 1977.

———*The On-Line Revolution in Libraries*. New York: Marcel Dekker, 1978.

———*Structure and Governance of Library Networks*. New York: Marcel Dekker, 1979.

Kerlinger, Fred N. *Foundations of Behavioral Research*. New York: Holt, Rinehart and Winston, 1973.

Kiechel, Walter III. "Everything You Always Wanted to Know May Soon Be On-Line." *Fortune* 101 (May 5, 1980): 226-240.

Kochen, Manfred. "Technology and Communication in the Future." *Journal of the American Society for Information Science* 32 (March 1981):148-157.

Korek, Michael, and Ray Olszewski. "Telecom: The Winds of Change." *Datamation* 27 (May 1981):160, 162, 164.

Kotler, Philip. *Marketing for Nonprofit Organizations*. Englewood Cliffs, N. J.: Prentice-Hall, 1975.

Kraemer, Kenneth, et al. *The Management of Information Systems*. New York: Columbia University Press, 1981.

Lancaster, F. W. "Whither Libraries? or Wither Libraries." *College and Research Libraries* 39 (September 1978): 345-57.

Lancaster, F. W., and Smith, Linda C. "On-Line Systems in the Communication Process: Projections." *Journal of the American Society for Information Science* 31 (May 1980):193-200.

Leavitt, Harold. *Managerial Psychology 4th ed*. Chicago: University of Chicago Press, 1978.

Lenk, J. D. *Handbook of Microprocessors, Microcomputers and Minicomputers*. Englewood Cliffs, N. J.: Prentice-Hall, 1979.

Levine, Arthur. "Management Information Systems: 'The New MIS' ". *Infosystems* 28 (September 1981):124-26.

Levine, Ronald D. "Supercomputers." *Scientific American* (January 1982):118-135.

Lindsay, Peter H., and Norman, Donald A. *Human Information Processing* 2nd ed. New York: Academic Press, 1977.

Line, Maurice B. "Libraries and Information Services in a Post-Technology Society." *Journal of Library Automation* 14 (December 1981):252-267.

Logsdon, Thomas S. *Computers and Social Controversy*. Potomac, Md.: Computer Science Press, 1980.

Long, Philip L. "Computer Technology—An Update." *Annual Review of Information Science and Technology* 11 (1976): 212-22.

Loomis, Mary E. S. "The Changing Nature of DBMS." *Infosystems* 9 (September 1981):67-72.

Machlup, Fritz. *The Production and Distribution of Knowledge*. Princeton, N.J.: Princeton University Press, 1962.

Maranjian, Lorig and Boss, Richard. *Fee-Based Information Services: A Study of a Growing Industry*. New York: R. R. Bowker, 1980.

Marsten, R. B., ed. *Communication Satellite Systems Technology*. New York: Academic Press, 1966.

Martin, James. *Communications Satellite Systems*. Englewood Cliffs, N.J.: Prentice-Hall, 1978.

———*Design and Strategy for Distributed Data Processing*. Englewood Cliffs, N.J.: Prentice-Hall, 1981.

———*Design of Man-Computer Dialogues*. Englewood Cliffs, N.J.: Prentice-Hall, 1973.

———*Future Developments in Telecommunications*. Englewood Cliffs, N.J.: Prentice-Hall, 1977.

———*Telematic Society: A Challenge for Tomorrow.* Englewood Cliffs, N.J.: Prentice-Hall, 1981.
Maslow, A. H. *Motivation and Personality.* New York: Harper and Row, 1954.
McKenney, James L., and McFarlan, F. Warren. "The Information Archipelago—Maps and Bridges." *Harvard Business Review* 60 (September-October 1982):109-119.
Mead, Carver, and Conway, Lynn. *Introduction to VLSI Systems.* Reading, Mass.: Addison-Wesley, 1980.
Miller, A.R. "Computers and Copyright Law." *Michigan State Bar Journal* 46 (April 1967):11-18.
Miller, Frederick W. "Mini vs. Mainframe: Who's Doing Whose Job." *Infosystems* 28 (May 1981):64, 72, 74.
———"*Navigating Through DBMS Software.*" *Infosystems* 28 (March 1981):70, 72, 74.
Murdick, Robert G. *MIS Concepts and Design.* Englewood Cliffs, N.J.: Prentice-Hall, 1980.
Myers, Edith. "The Floppy Is Here." *Datamation* 27(August 1981):92-94.
NATO Advanced Study Institute on Perspectives in Information Science. Leyden: Noordhoff, 1975.
Newell, Allen, and Simon, Herbert. *Human Problem Solving.* Englewood Cliffs, N.J.: Prentice-Hall, 1972.
Nolan, Richard. "Managing Crises in Data Processing." *Harvard Business Review* 57 (March-April, 1979):115-116.
———"*Managing Information Systems by Committee.*" *Harvard Business Review* 60 (July-August 1982): 72-79.
Ouchi, William G. *Theory Z: How American Business Can Meet the Japanese Challenge.* Reading, Mass.: Addison-Wesley, 1981.
Personal Privacy in an Information Society: The Report of the Privacy Protection Study Committee, July 1977. Washington, D.C.: U.S. Government Printing Office, 1977.
Petersohn, Henry. "Management of Information Resources." *Information and Records Management* 15 (September 1981):65-66.
Poppel, Harvey L. "The Information Revolution: Winners and Losers." *Harvard Business Review* 56 (January-February 1978):14-16 & 159.
Porat, Marc Uri. *The Information Economy.* Washington, D.C.: U.S. Government Printing Office, 1977.
Pratt, Allan D. "The Use of Microcomputers in Libraries." *Journal of Library Automation* 13 (March 1980):7-17.
Raffin, M., ed. *The Marketing of Information Services, Proceedings Seminar. Aslib Information Industry Group, May 11, 1977.* London: Aslib, 1978.
Ranftl, Robert M. "Productivity—A Critical Challenge of the 1980s." *Infosystems* 26 (October 1979):55-70.

Rhodes, Wayne L. "Information Systems Management: A Hybrid Blossoms." *Infosystems* 28 (January 1981):32-36.
──── "Office of the Future, Light Years Away?" *Infosystems* 28 (March 1981):40-50.
──── "Time is a Tightrope: A Day in the Life of an MIS Manager." *Infosystems* 29 (January 1982):34-38.
"The Right to Privacy in Nineteenth Century America." *Harvard Law Review* 94 (June 1981).
Robinson, Barbara M. "Cooperation and Competition among Library Networks." *Journal of the American Society for Information Science* 31 (November 1980):413-24.
Rockhold, Alan. "Bottom-line Report: Protecting the Computer Environment." *Infosystems* 29 (January 1982):64, 66, 68 & 70.
──── "*Fiber Optics*: A New World of Communications." *Infosystems* 28 (August 1981):56-62.
──── "Keep to Successful Office Automation: Company Strategies and User Needs." *Infosystems* 29 (March 1982):66-72.
Rosen, S. "Electronic Computers: A Historical Survey." *Computing Surveys* 1 (March 1969):8-36.
Saffady, William. *The Automated Office.* Silver Springs, Md.: National Micrographics Association, 1981.
Salton, Gerard. "A Progress Report on Information Privacy and Data Security." *Journal of the American Society for Information Science* 31 (March 1980):75-83.
Satyanarayanan, M. *Multiprocessors: A Comparative Study.* Englewood Cliffs, N.J.: Prentice-Hall, 1980.
Shaw, Alan C. *The Logical Design of Operating Systems.* Englewood Cliffs, N.J.: Prentice-Hall, 1974.
Simon, Herbert Alexander. *The New Science of Management Decision.* Englewood Cliffs, N.J.: Prentice-Hall, 1977.
──── *The Science of the Artificial.* Cambridge Mass.: MIT Press, 1969.
Sippl, Charles J. *The Essential Computer Dictionary and Speller.* Englewood Cliffs, N.J.: Prentice-Hall, 1980.
Smith, Robert E. "Privacy Still Threatened." *Datamation* (September 1982):297-306.
Sojka, Deborah, and Dorn, Phillip H. "Magic Moments in Software." *Datamation* 27 (August 1981):7-16.
Stanton, William. *Fundamentals of Marketing.* New York: McGraw-Hill, 1981.
Sterns, Peter M. "Is There a Post-Industrial Society?" *Society* 11 (1974).
Stibbens, Steve. "There's No Place Like Home: The Personal Computer Has Come Home." *Infosystems* 28 (December 1981):38, 40, 42.
Stonecash, J. C. "The IRM Showdown." *Infosystems* 28 (October 1981):42-48.

Stoneman, Paul. *Technological Diffusion and the Computer Revolution: The U.K. Experience.* Cambridge University Press, 1976.

Szuprowicz, Bohdan O. "The World's Top 50 Computer Import Markets." *Datamation* 27 (January 1981):14, 144.

Thiel, Carol Tomme. "Programming Tools: Impacting DP Productivity." *Infosystems* 29 (March 1982):56-60.

Veith, Richard H. "Informatics and Transborder Data Flow: The Question of Social Impact." *Journal of the American Society for Information Science* 31 (March 1980): 105-110.

Venenziano, Velma. "Library Automation: Data for Processing and Processing for Data." *Annual Review of Information Science and Technology* 15 (1980):109-145.

Verity, John W. "Wall Street Wed to Software." *Datamation* 27 (August 1981):53-56.

Wagner, Judy. "Data Base Management System Design for Library Automation." *Journal of Library Automation* 13 (March 1980):56-61.

Warren, S. D., and Brandeis, L. D. "The Right to Privacy." *Harvard Law Review* 4(5)(December 15, 1890):193-220.

Weizer, Norman. "A History of Operating Systems." *Datamation* 27 (January 1981):118-26.

Wessel, Andrew. *The Social Use of Information Ownership and Access.* New York: Wiley-Interscience, 1976.

Whinston, Andrew B., and Holsapple, C. W. "DBMs for Micros." *Datamation* 27 (April 1981):165-67.

The White House Conference on Library and Information Services, Washington, D.C. 1979. Information for the 1980s. Washington, D.C.: Government Printing Office, 1980.

Williams, James G. "Information Technology—A State of the Art." Unpublished Paper Presented to the 1981 Pittsburgh Conference: The Challenge of Change—Critical Choices for Library Decision Makers (November 2-4, 1981).

Williams, M. E., et al. *Computer-Readable Databases—A Directory and Data Sourcebook.* White Plains, N.Y.: Knowledge Industry Publications, 1982.

Williams, P. W., and Goldsmith, G. "Information Retrieval on Mini and Microcomputers." *Annual Review of Information Science and Technology* 16 (1981):85-111.

Wilson, T. D. "On User Studies and Information Needs." *Journal of Documentation* 37 (March 1981):3-15.

Withington, F. G. "Computer Technology: State of the Art." *Journal of the American Society for Information Science* 32 (March 1981):124-30.

———"Coping with Computer Proliferation." *Harvard Business Review* 58 (May-June 1980):152-64.

Yasaki, Edward K. "Tokyo Looks to the 90s." *Datamation* 28 (January 1982):110-115.

Yourdon, Edward. *Design of On-Line Computer Systems.* Englewood Cliffs, N.J.: Prentice-Hall, 1972.

Zais, H. W. *Economic Modelling: An Aid to the Pricing of Information Services.* Berkeley: Lawrence Berkeley Laboratory, University of California, 1976.

Zimmerman, Mark D. "Japan Throws Down the Computer Gauntlet." *Machine Design* 54 (February 1982):22, 24.

Index

Aaker, David A., 134
Accelerated obsolescence in information technology: remedies of, 162
Acceptance of fees: analysis, 146-160
Accessibility to vital information, during the Information Age, 161
Amdahl, 163
Animated tellers: in banks, 124
Apple Computers, 163; Apple II, 32
Arithmetic Logic Unit, 21
ARPANET, 38
Artandi, Susan, 5, 91, 94
AT&T: data communications services, 125; Yellow Pages, 83
Audio/video equipment: in office automation, 121
Automation: definition, 43; closed-loop concept, 43; incentives for, 47, 49; office, 57-58; of library, 50; negative influences, 48
Average Total Cost: definition, 111

Bacon, Donald C., 100
Bandwagon effect, the: dangers of in office automation, 162
Bell, Daniel, 3, 4

Bell Laboratories, 22
Bibliotheque Nationale, La (Paris): as a major information source, 93
Bodleian library (Oxford University), 93
Brandeis, Louis D., 100
Break even point analysis: as an aid in pricing, 116
Break even point: calculation in cost recovery, 112
Bush, Vennevar, 16
The Business of Information Report, 10

Cable television. See CATV
CAD. See Computer assisted design
CAD/CAM and robotics unit: functions, 124
CAM. See Computer assisted manufacturing
Canadian On-Line Enquiry, 12
CAN-OLE. See Canadian On-Line Enquiry
Cases in information marketing research, 137-160
Cathode ray tube. See CRT
CATV, 39
Central processor, 21

188 Index

Cogswell, James A., 95, 97
COM. *See* Computer Output Microfilm
Communications networks: in information processing, 119
Competition based pricing method, 108, 116
Compunications, 38, 119
Computer assisted design and manufacturing: association with engineering design, 120
Computer-based data banks, 102; and copyright law, 99; and individual privacy, 100; competition with libraries, 94; and information imperialism, 87; and user access, 93
Computer-based reprography, 119; reprographic unit, functions, 121
Computer-based information centers: in corporations, 83; networks, improved performance, 162; Resource Sharing Networks, 54
Computer-based services: in public libraries, 138; in university libraries, 139
Computer components, 21
Computer generations, 18-24; table, 20
Computer output on microfilm, 121
Computer Output Microfilm, 34
Computers, personal, 10
Computer programs and copyright law, 99
Connell, John J., 119
Consumer behavior: assessment techniques, 109
Control unit, 21
Conway, Lynn, 32
Coordination: of information technologies, 124-125
Copyright Act of 1909, 99; of 1976, 98-99

Copyright law, 98-99
Corporate data banks, and privacy legislation, 101
Corporation information systems, 51-54; management, 53; manufacturing industries, 51
Cost based pricing, 107-112
Cost concepts, 111; cost recovery, in price fixing, 112
CPU. *See* Central processing unit
Crisis management function: in information resources management, 127
CRT, 37

Data analysis: in information marketing research, 137
Data banks, accelerated growth of, 163
Database management systems: use in accessing central data banks, 124
Database: information pricing, 106; producers, 75; vendors, competition with government agencies, 97
Data communications and networks, 37-39; relationship with telecommunications, 120; unit, functions, 121
Data entry and display, 37
Data processing services: user needs, 73; providers, 73
Data processing unit: functions of, 121
Data Resources Inc., sales forecasts, 88
Day, George S., 134
Debons, Anthony, 4
Decision making: and information, 84; models, and information inputs, 85
DeGennaro, Richard, 48, 95, 96

Demand based pricing, 116; method, 107
Democratic party: and information power, 88
Design implementation: in information marketing research, 137
DIALIB, 138-139; user fees study, 97
DIALOG, online system, 83, 139
Diebold, John, 47
Discounts: in pricing strategy, 117
Distributed processing, 24; problems in information resource management, 126
Dow Jones News Retrieval Online Service, 75
Dragon, Andrea C., 109

Eastman Kodak: as Theory Z organization, 129
Eckert, J. Presper, 22
Econometric Models: in information pricing, 107; in price theory, 105
Elections: information power role in, 88
Electronic fund transfer (EFT): demand in home terminal survey, 1980-81, 138
Electronic mail, 10; in office automation, 162
ENIAC, 22
Ergonomics, 37
EURONET. See European Computer Network
European Computer Network, 11
European Economic Community, 11

Facsimile productions, 121
Facsimile transmission: in office automation, 58, 162
Fair use determination, 99
Fair use doctrine, 99
FAX. See Facsimile

Federal data banks, 100; and privacy, 100-101
Federal Register, 83
Fee-based Information Service Centers in Academic Libraries (FISCAL), 106
Fees: as a deterrent to information use, 142
Fees controversy, 93-97, 101
Fees for information: arguments against, 96; arguments for, 96-97
Fifth generation computers: features, 162; Japanese research, 24
FISCAL. See Fee-based Information Service Centers in Academic Libraries
Fixed cost, definition, 111
FIOA. See Freedom of Information Act
Freedom of Information Act (FOIA): exemptions, 100; of 1966, 7, 99-100
Free library service: as an American tradition, 96
Froehlich, Leopold, 64
Frohman, Alan L., 64

Garfield, Eugene, 96
Garvin, Andrew P., 5, 53, 74, 87
GATT: role in international information transfer, 162
General Agreement on Tariffs and Trade. See GATT
Gilpin, Alan, 65
Growth function: information technological, 16

Hardware: evolving industry characteristics, 163; growth rates, 68; types of, 66
Hewlett-Packard: as Theory Z organization, 129
Hierarchy of needs, Maslow's, 89

Home automation, 59-60; developmental requirements, 59; services, 59
Home computer services, 138
Home terminal survey, 1980-81, 138
Horton, Forest Woody, Jr., 53, 127
Human factors: in user access to information, 163
Human resources allocation function, 126
Huskey, Harry D., 15

IBM: as Theory Z organization, 129
Information: as commodity, 5; and decision making, 84; definition of, 4; obstacles to acquisition of, 6-8; problems of interdependence, 11; relationship to knowledge, 4; seminal dimensions, 8; as a source of power in business, 87; as a survival tool, 101-102; and user needs, 91
Information brokers: competition with government agencies, 97; competition with libraries, 94; and information pricing, 106; marketing problems, 110
Information centers: and libraries, 49; similarities in corporations and research libraries, 45-46
Information consultants: competition with libraries, 94
Information coordination unit functions, 123, 126
Information data banks: and information pricing, 106; and user access, 93
Information imperialism: in business, 87
Information industry, 65-76; private sector, 65-66; public sector, 65
Information Industry Association, 79-80; *The Business of Information Report*, 10
Information market: definition, 77; segmentation, 77; industrial market, 78; consumer market, 78-79
Information marketing: definition, 133
Information market operators, 79
Information monopoly: in the Information Age, 88; and power, 84-85
Information need: in information transfer, 91
Information networks: in institutions, 121; in party politics, 88; performance evaluation of, 127
Information policy: development in organizations, 125
Information power: and access to information, 89; in party politics, 88
Information processing technologies: in management, 119
Information product: design, 109; quality control, 120
Information professionals: and user needs, 84
Information resources: management function, 120; organization structures, 129-132
Information revolution, factors causing, 6
Information seeking behavior: and motivation for seeking information, 84, 89
Information services, 72
Information technologies: coordination, 124-125; growth and decline in DP manager's power, 120
Information value: difficulty of assessment, 110-111; disregard by demand based pricing, 116; volatile nature of, 91
Input device, 21
Institutional information network components, 121

Integrated circuit, 23
INTEL Corporation: first microcomputer, 15
INTELSAT I, 38
Interactive graphics, 121
International barriers to information flow, 161

Kelly, Orr, 100
Kerlinger, Fred N., 141
King, Hulas H., 52
King Research Inc.: investigation of pricing methods, 106
Kirchner, Englebert, 67
Klee, Kenneth, 52
Korek, Michael, 9
Kotler, Philip, 108, 111
Kuehl, Philip G., 111
Kusler, Alan, 95

Lancaster, Wildred F., 50, 51
Leavitt, Harold, 84
Legal issues: in user access to information, 98-101
LEXIS online system, 74, 83
Library of Congress, 124; as a major information source, 93
Library technology, 119
Lindsay, Peter H., 90
Line, Maurice, 50
Lockheed Information Retrieval System, 107
Loveless, Stephen, 121
Lombardo, Rita, 11
Long, Philip L., 15
LSI (Large Scale Integrated Circuits), 24, 32

McGowan, Robert P., 121
McGregor, Douglas, 128
Machlup, Fritz, 4; research at Princeton University, 9
Macro information systems, 93

Magnetic tape, 34
Magnuson, 163
Mailing lists, 101; and privacy law, regulation, 101
Mainframes: characteristics, 26
Management: functions, in information resource management, 125; information systems, 52; style, in information resources management, 127; theories, 127-132
Marginal Cost: definition, 111
Market segmentation, 109
Marketing concept: and client emphasis, 108; in price theory, 107; and user satisfaction, 109
Marketing principles, in information pricing, 106, 108; attracting tax dollars, 110; promotion, 109
Marketing research: definition, 134; issues in the Information Age, 164-165; procedure, 134-137; steps in, 135
Markuson, Barbara E., 49
Martin, James, 18
Maslow, Abraham, 89, 90
Massachusetts Institute of Technology. See M.I.T.
Mass storage, 32-34
Material resources allocation function, 126
Mauchly, John W., 22
M'bow, Ahmadou-Mahtar, 12
Mead, Carver, 32
Mead Corporation. See LEXIS
Medical Literature Analysis and Retrieval System. See MEDLARS
MEDLARS, 107, 111
MEDLINE (online medical information system), 7, 83, 95, 139
Meserve, Evrett, 10
Metal Oxide Semiconductor, 15, 32
Microcomputer, 32, 72; characteristics, 70; in office automation, 162

Milcro information systems: and user access, 92
Microwave data communication: increased use of, 162
Miller, Frederick W., 25
Minicomputers, 26
M.I.T.: study of computer-based reference services, 139; user fees study, 97
MOS. *See* Metal Oxide Semiconductor
Moses, Joel, 60
MTBF (Mean Time Between Failures), 60
MTTR (Mean Time To Repair), 60
Multiprocessing, 24
Multiprogramming, 24
Murray, Robert, 124

NASA, role in data base development, 98
NASIC. *See* Northeast Academic Science Information Center
National Aeronautical and Space Administration. *See* NASA
National Commission on Libraries and Information Services (NCLIS), 96
National Information Conference and Exposition, 11
National Library of Medicine: role in database development, 98, 139; suit brought against by System Development Corporation, 7
National Science Foundation, 50, 139; role in database development, 98; sponsor of DIALIB (1974-1977), 138
NCC (National Computer Conference), 68
Nets. See Network
Network, 54; architecture, 55; elements, 55; figure, 56; reasons for, 55
Newell, Allen, 90
New York Public Library: as a major information source, 93
Nice. *See* National Information Conference and Exposition
NLM. *See* National Library of Medicine
Nolan, Richard, 127
Norman, Donald A., 90
Norris, William, 119
Northeast Academic Science Information Center (NASIC), 139

Oates, James, 91
OCLC (Online Computer Library Center), 48-49
OCR (optical character recognition), 37
Office automation: contents, 121; definition, 57; eight major elements, 57
Olszewski, Ray, 9
Online database, 74; as premium information sources, 85; services: 73-77, modes of operation, 75, table of, 76
Optical Character Reader. *See* OCR
Optimum pricing of information, 107, 117
Organization structure: in information resource management, 126, 129-132
OS. *See* Software
Ouchi, William G., 128, 129
Output Device, 22

Paperwork Reduction Act of 1980, 9
Payment Systems Inc., home terminal survey, 1980-81, 138
Pearson, A.W., 91
People management concept, in in-

formation resources management, 128
Performance evaluation, of information networks, 127
Personal information: in computer-based data banks, 101
Personality and motivation, Maslow's theory on, 89
Pittsburgh (Pennsylvania) Study of information use, 110, 139-160; areas of specialty, 142; categories of users, 159-160; considerations of:
  age, 144; education, 145; income, 145; marital status, 144; sex, 142;
  data analysis, 146-160; findings, 157-160; hypotheses, 140, 158-159; Likert-type questionnaire, 140; participation in funded project, 142; personal interview, 156
Poppel, Harvey L., 53
Predicasts Inc.: Promt online database, 88
Price discrimination, 108; legal restrictions of, 117; theory, 105, 107-108
Pricing: alternatives for non profit organizations, 117; goals, definition, 107; methods: 107-108, and equity in information handling, 164; and government regulations, 108;
  objectives, 107; principles, 105, 106; strategy, 108, 117
Primary Storage Unit, 21
Privacy Act: restrictions in accessing central data banks, 125
Privacy Act of 1974, 100
Privacy Law, 100-101; and mailing lists, 101
Privacy Protection Study Commission Report of 1977, 101

Productivity: as a function of information management, 164; importance of information technology in, 119
Problem solving, and information, 84
Promt, 88
Punched cards, 34
Purpose identification: in information marketing research, 135

Quality control: of information products, 120

Recovery rate, 60
Redwood City Public Library, 139
Republican party: and information power, 88
Research design: in information marketing research, 137
Resource sharing, 54
R.L. Polk & Co.: mailing lists, 101
Robinson-Patman Act of 1936, 117
Robotics: in information processing, 119
Runaway technology phemonenon: and technological change, 85

Saffady, William, 57
Salmere, Mitchel, 53
San Jose Public Library, 139
San Mateo County Library, 139
Santa Clara County Library, 139
Satisficing decision model, 84
Satellite data communications: and improvements in data flow, 162
Scheffes S method, for statistical analysis, 147
SDC. *See* Systems Development Corporation
Security of personal information: need for enforcement of, 164
Seductive information systems de-

signs, for user maximum satisfaction, 165
SCORPIO, Library of Congress online catalog, 124
Shapiro, Benson D., 108
Silicon chip, 23
Silicon Valley, 17
Simon, Herbert, 45, 52, 90
Social Security computer system, 101; data bank, 100
Societal information systems, 83; and Freedom of Information Act, 100; as information sources, 84; and user access, 93
Software: definition, 39, 71, categories, 39; functions, 39; OS, 39; sector, increasing its share of the information industry, 163; trends, 39
Strategic planning: for information resource management, 124; in the public sector, 121; relationship with marketing research, 134
Suprenant, Tom, 50
System designers: and user access, 92
Systems Development Corporation: suit against National Library of Medicine, 7, 139
System reliability: backups and security, 60

Technological change: effect of runaway technology phenomenon, 85
Teleconferencing, 58, 121, 162
TELENET, data communications services, 125
Teletypes, 37
Theory X, 127-129
Theory Y, 127-129
Theory Z, 127-129
Theory Z organizations, 129
Total Cost: definition, 111

Total Fixed Cost: definition, 111
Total Variable Cost: definition, 111
Transborder data flow: in the Information Age, 162
Transistors, 23
Treasury Department: data bank, 101
TYMNET, data communications services, 125

UNESCO: role in international information transfer, 12, 162
United Nations Educational, Scientific and Cultural Organization. See UNESCO
United Nations Organization: role in international information transfer, 161
Universal Product Code (UPC), 37
University of Pennsylvania: user fees study, 97
UPC. See Universal Product Code
U.S. Department of Commerce, 63; 1977 study of the information economy, 8
U.S. Department of Health and Human Services: data bank, 100
U.S. military: as Theory Z Organization, 129
User access to information, 84; scope, 92
User attitudes: toward comprehensive manual literature search services, 147; toward inter library loans, 147-148
User fees, 139; studies, 97
User friendly information systems, 92, 164
User needs: of individuals, 89, 91; identification, 84; Maslow's hierarchy of, 89; of organizations, 91; primacy in information handling, 109

Vacuum tube, 22
Variable cost, definition, 111
Verity, John, 69
Very Large Scale Integrated Circuits. *See* VLSI
Virtual memory, 24
VLSI, 19, 24-25

Wang Laboratories, 163
Warren, Samuel D., 100
Weinstock, M., 110

White House Conference on Library and Information Services, 12, 88
Williams, James G., 37
Williams, Martha, 75, 98
Wilson, T.D., 90
Withington, Frederic G., 58
Word processing, 119, 120
Word processors: in office automation, 121

Zais, Harriet W., 117

About the Author

HARRY M. KIBIRIGE is Senior Programmer-Analyst and Head of Microcomputer Applications at the University of Pittsburgh. He has contributed articles to *International Library Review*, *UNESCO Bulletin for Libraries*, *Libri*, and the *ALA Encyclopedia of Library and Information Services*, among others.